Californian Indian Nights

MEDICINE MAN, OR SHAMAN, OF THE POMO INDIANS, CALIFORNIA
Conducting a ceremony over a deceased tribesman

Californian Indian Nights

Stories of the creation of the world, of
man, of fire, of the sun, of thunder,
etc.; of coyote, the land of the
dead, the sky land, mon-
sters, animal people, etc.

compiled by

EDWARD WINSLOW GIFFORD

and

GWENDOLINE HARRIS BLOCK

Introduction to the Bison Book Edition by Albert L. Hurtado

University of Nebraska Press
Lincoln and London

First Bison Book printing: 1990
Most recent printing indicated by the last digit below:
10   9   8   7   6   5   4   3   2   1

Library of Congress Cataloging-in-Publication Data
Gifford, Edward Winslow, 1887–
[Californian Indian nights entertainments]
Californian Indian nights: stories of the creation of the world, of
fire, of the sun, of thunder . . . / compiled by Edward W. Gifford and
Gwendoline Harris Block; introduction by Albert L. Hurtado.—1st Bison
book print.
p.   cm.
Selected and adapted for a popular audience from various academic publications—Cf. Introd.
Reprint. Originally published: Californian Indian nights entertainments.
Glendale, Calif., U.S.A.: A. H. Clark Co., 1930.
ISBN 0-8032-7031-3
1. Indians of North America—California—Religion and mythology.   2. Indians of North America—California—Legends.   I. Block, Gwendoline Harris.   II. Title.
E78.C15G397   1990
398.2'089970794—dc20
90-33808   CIP

Reprinted by arrangement with the Arthur H. Clark Company

Originally published as *Californian Indian Nights Entertainments*

Contents

Illustrations

clapper-rattle, wears on his head a netting cap full of goose down, across his forehead a brilliant salmon-pink head-band made of flicker feathers and over his shoulders a netting cape with hawk feathers attached.

Introduction to the Bison Book Edition
Albert L. Hurtado

During the first decades of the twentieth century the University of California became renowned for its department of anthropology. Although scholars contributed to many fields of anthropological science, the department was best known for studies of California Indians. While Alfred Kroeber guided these developments, a host of colleagues and students joined him to make California Indians the most thoroughly studied native people in North America.[1]

Two of these Berkeley scholars compiled the present volume of California Indian stories. Edward Winslow Gifford (1887–1959) is the best known. Author of more than one hundred publications, professor at Berkeley, and director of the University of California Museum of Anthropology, Gifford was a respected and highly visible member of the anthropological profession.[2] Gwendoline Harris Block (1906–1956), on the other hand, was far less conspicuous.[3] She worked in clerical and administrative positions at the university, and this book is her only publication.

When Gifford came to work at the Museum of Anthropology as assistant curator in 1912 he had interesting but unconventional academic credentials. A graduate of an Oakland, California, high school, Gifford did not attend college, but at eighteen took a job as assistant curator in the California Academy of Science's department of ornithology. In 1905 he accompanied the academy's expedition to the Galapagos Islands where he observed the behavior of a species of finch that used twigs to pry insects from tree bark. His published report of this tool-making bird was not given much credence by established ornithologists until 1940, when motion pictures confirmed Gifford's precocious account.

After Gifford joined the staff of the university museum he assumed increased responsibility, much to the delight of Kroeber, who sought relief from administrative and curatorial chores. In 1915 Gifford was advanced to associate curator, and in 1925 became curator of the museum. His designation as museum director in 1947 merely recognized the executive authority he had exercised for many years. Gifford had more than technical and administrative talents, and despite his lack of college training the university gave him an academic appointment in 1920. In 1945 he was promoted to professor of anthropology. During his long and distinguished career, Gifford worked in Oceania, Yap, Mexico, and New Caledonia. His principal interest in California Indians resulted in publications that are still basic to the field.[4]

In 1924 Gifford hired a new museum helper, Gwendoline Harris, who was fresh out of high school. She attended night school to learn stenography and earned promotion to assistant in anthropology. In 1929 she married Coleman Block, a San Francisco physician, and resigned, but returned to the museum in 1931. Soon the anthropology department recognized her intellectual ability, and she began routinely to edit the department's publications, an assignment that was formally recognized when she was named editor in anthropology in 1938. Altogether, Block edited seventy-six monographs in three University of California Press series, *Publications in American Archaeology and Ethnology, Anthropological Records,* and *Ibero-Americana.* She also edited *Essays in Anthropology Presented to A. L. Kroeber in Honor of His Sixtieth Birthday.*[5] Kroeber displayed his respect for her contribution to Berkeley's Department of Anthropology by writing her obituary for the *American Anthropologist.*

Block and Gifford published *Californian Indian Nights Entertainments* in 1930 during her brief hiatus in university employment. They intended their book for a popular audience and selected and adapted these tales accordingly. Many of the stories had previously been printed in various academic publications where fidelity to Indian linguistic forms and ethnographic accuracy were the main considerations. Block and Gifford edited the stories to give them broader appeal without unduly damaging their authenticity. For example, they eliminated repetition, a common rhetorical device in Indian oratory.

Although the stories were the main focus of the book, the compilers knew that lay readers would need some background on California Indian culture. Consequently, they composed a sixty-page introduction that encapsulated then current anthropological knowledge. Understandably, in the ensuing sixty years there have been advances in the field, but on the whole their introduction still stands up. Readers who want to expand their knowledge of California Indian culture should refer to the recent work of California anthropologists.[6]

Modern readers should be aware of a few of the idiosyncrasies in the original introduction. The word *Indian* was spelled with a lower case "i," no doubt a stylistic convention imposed by the publisher. And occasionally Gifford and Block use the word *primitive* to describe Indian culture. The introduction disparages what little Indian pottery existed in California but fails to mention the exceedingly fine basketry that was found throughout the state. The authors also understate the average size of Indian communities in Central California as about one hundred. Now it is believed that, though the smallest villages were about that size, many large towns had one thousand or more people.[7]

The Indian population of California is an important matter that has inspired debate among scholars. Gifford and Block do not discuss it, aside from the average size of villages, but they probably believed Kroeber's estimate of approximately 133,000 Indians at the time of Spanish settlement in 1769. Now the appraisal of the Berkeley demographer Sherburne F. Cook—about 310,000—is widely accepted. By 1900 the Indian population had fallen to about 21,000.[8] The preface to the original edition vaguely refers to this rapid and tragic depletion of Indians near the missions with the phrase "early extinction or Mexicanization," but the authors do not explain the causes of these developments. This is not surprising since only the bare outline of California Indian history was then known.

A much more detailed picture of Indian history has emerged since this book was first published. The Spanish Empire had long relied on missions as a means of pacifying the Indians in its extensive colonial possessions, and California was not exceptional. Beginning in 1769, Franciscan missionaries founded twenty-one missions along the California coast from San Diego to Sonoma. The friars intended to Hispanicize and convert the Indians while eliminating any vestiges of native culture that did not conform to Catholic dogma. Once the missionaries had tutored the neophytes—the term Spaniards applied to mission Indians— they could enter Spanish society as laborers. This melding of religious fervor and expedience had mixed results on the California frontier. Spanish missionaries, soldiers, and settlers brought new diseases as well as novel religious and cultural ideas. Sickness swept through mission populations and killed thousands of neophytes. Even though missions were confined to the coast, diseases spread inland and claimed victims among the unconverted tribes. By the end of the Hispanic era only about 150,000 Indians remained in California.[9]

In the meantime, California Indians responded to the Spanish incursion and demographic decline in a variety of ways. Some chose peaceful accommodation to mission life; others rebelled against colonial authority and embarked on careers as livestock raiders. Many raiders were former neophytes who fled the missions and established themselves among tribes—especially the Miwok and Yokuts—in the San Joaquin Valley. The horse became central to their way of life, and their forays against mission herds were a troublesome reality for Spanish priests and soldiers. These raids continued after Mexican independence in 1821, which brought about the secularization of the missions and the rise of great, privately owned land-grant ranchos in California.[10]

Indian-white relations changed dramatically in 1846 when the United States conquered California during the Mexican War. The Hispanic era had been a demographic disaster for California Indians, but the years of the gold rush under the aegis of the United States would be even worse. Beginning in 1848, thousands of miners swarmed over Indian lands and appropriated whatever they wanted. Now a majority, whites attacked native communities, killing or driving away any who offered resistance. These assaults killed an unknown number of Indians and forced the survivors to live in marginal areas where subsistence was difficult to obtain. Malnutrition, starvation, disease, and early death were the results.[11]

By 1860 only about thirty thousand Indians remained in California. The destruction of California Indians eliminated whole tribes and left only a remnant population with knowledge of traditional life before the arrival of Europeans. Scholars began to study Indian survivors in the late nineteenth century, but systematic investigation by trained anthropologists dates from 1900, when Kroeber arrived.[12] The extensive ethnographic work of Kroeber, Gifford, and many others resulted in the accumulation of hundreds of stories that illuminate Indian culture and history. It was these firsthand accounts that Gifford and Block culled for the present book, opening a window on the lost world of Indian life and belief before the arrival of Europeans more than two centuries ago. It was a world of impressive dimensions and powerful imagination—a place peopled with grand mythic characters, figures who were part human and part animal. Here we find the ubiquitous Coyote, the trickster, forever making trouble. There are many common themes in these stories, but in keeping with California's cultural heterogeneity, there is great variety, too. Each tribe had its own version of how the earth was created. Some believed that the world was made from the sand under the nails of a great turtle who dived beneath a limitless sea; others thought that a world maker had fashioned it from basket work. Many of the stories have a moral dimension that tells us about the Indians' ethical sense. Others convey religious ideas. And some are just good stories that are told for the joy of telling and the wonder of listening.

The joy and wonder are still present in this record of Indian oral traditions that transcend the horror of nineteenth-century carnage and vividly remind us of California's cultural richness and diversity. For those who wish to know about the Indians of California there is no more enjoyable way to begin than with this book. This collection of stories conveys the uniqueness of Indian society, and also affirms the human identity of the narrators who wonder about life, death, right, wrong, and the origins of humankind. The Indians who lived to tell these tales testified also to the ability of people to persist in the harshest of circumstances. This book is a tribute to the Indians who survived a harrowing time and to the anthropologists who cared enough to write down their stories, especially Edward Winslow Gifford and Gwendoline Harris Block.

NOTES

1. Robert F. Heizer, "History of Research," in *Handbook of North American Indians,* vol. 8, *California,* ed. Heizer (Washington, D.C. 1978), pp. 9–10; Timothy H. H. Thoresen, "Paying the Piper and Calling the Tune: The Beginnings of Academic Anthropology in California," *Journal of the History of the Behavioral Sciences* 11 (July 1975): 257–75; Theodora Kroeber, *Alfred Kroeber, A Personal Configuration* (Berkeley: University of California Press, 1970), pp. 93–94.

2. George M. Foster, "Edward Winslow Gifford," *American Anthropologist* 62 (April 1960): 327–29.

3. See her obituary by Alfred L. Kroeber: "Gwendoline Harris Block," *American Anthropologist* 59 (February 1957): 125.

4. Foster, "Gifford," 327–28.

5. As is customary, Block's role as copy editor was not formally noted on the title page. Instead, anthropologist Robert Lowie is named as editor of the essays in honor of Kroeber (Berkeley: University of California Press, 1936).

6. The best brief introduction is Robert F. Heizer and Albert B. Elsasser, *The Natural World of the California Indians* (Berkeley: University of California Press, 1980). An excellent collection of articles on California Indian culture, including four by Gifford, is R. F. Heizer and M. A. Whipple, eds., *The California Indians: A Source Book,* 2nd ed. (Berkeley: University of California Press, 1971). See also the encyclopedic *Handbook of North American Indians,* vol. 8, edited by Heizer.

7. Heizer and Elsasser, *Natural World,* p. 42.

8. Cook, *The Population of the California Indians, 1769–1970* (Berkeley: University of California Press, 1976), 43, 73; Albert L. Hurtado, "California Indian Demography, Sherburne F. Cook, and the Revision of American His-

tory," *Pacific Historical Review* 58 (August 1989): 323–43. See also Russell Thornton, *American Indian Holocaust and Survival: A Population History Since 1492* (Norman: University of Oklahoma Press, 1987), pp. 28–29.

9. Sherburne F. Cook, "The Indian Versus the Spanish Mission," in Cook, *The Conflict between the California Indian and White Civilization* (Berkeley: University of California Press, 1976), pp. 1–161; and Cook, *Population of the California Indians,* p. 44.

10. Albert L. Hurtado, *Indian Survival on the California Frontier* (New Haven: Yale University Press, 1988), pp. 32–54.

11. Hurtado, *Indian Survival,* pp. 100–218.

12. Heizer, "History of Research," pp. 7–8; Thoresen, "Paying the Piper and Calling the Tune," 263.

LOCATION OF NATIVE TRIBES, GROUPS, DIALECTS AND FAMILIES OF CALIFORNIA IN 1770

(See over for map.)

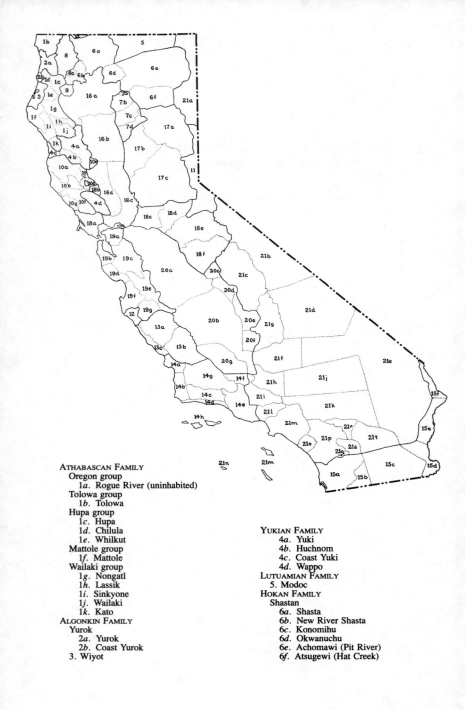

ATHABASCAN FAMILY
Oregon group
  1*a*. Rogue River (uninhabited)
Tolowa group
  1*b*. Tolowa
Hupa group
  1*c*. Hupa
  1*d*. Chilula
  1*e*. Whilkut
Mattole group
  1*f*. Mattole
Wailaki group
  1*g*. Nongatl
  1*h*. Lassik
  1*i*. Sinkyone
  1*j*. Wailaki
  1*k*. Kato
ALGONKIN FAMILY
Yurok
  2*a*. Yurok
  2*b*. Coast Yurok
3. Wiyot

YUKIAN FAMILY
  4*a*. Yuki
  4*b*. Huchnom
  4*c*. Coast Yuki
  4*d*. Wappo
LUTUAMIAN FAMILY
5. Modoc
HOKAN FAMILY
Shastan
  6*a*. Shasta
  6*b*. New River Shasta
  6*c*. Konomihu
  6*d*. Okwanuchu
  6*e*. Achomawi (Pit River)
  6*f*. Atsugewi (Hat Creek)

Yana
7a. Northern Yana (Noze)
7b. Central Yana (Noze)
7c. Southern Yana
7d. Yahi
8. Karok
9. Chimariko
Pomo
10a. Northern
10b. Central
10c. Eastern
10d. Southeastern
10e. Northeastern
10f. Southern
10g. Southwestern
11. Washo
12. Esselen
Salinan
13a. Antoniano
13b. Migueleño
13c. Playano (doubtful)
Chumash
14a. Obispeño
14b. Purisimeño
14c. Ynezeño
14d. Barbareño
14e. Ventureño
14f. Emigdiano
14g. Interior (doubtful)
14h. Island
Yuman
15a. Northern (Western) Diegueño
15b. Southern (Eastern) Diegueño
15c. Kamia
15d. Yuma
15e. Halchidhoma (now Chemehuevi)
15f. Mohave
PENUTIAN FAMILY
Wintun
  Dialect groups:
16a. Northern
16b. Central (Nomlaki)
16c. Southeastern (Patwin)
16d. Southwestern (Patwin)
Maidu
  Dialect groups:
17a. Northeastern
17b. Northwestern
17c. Southern (Nisenan)
Miwok
18a. Coast
18b. Lake
18c. Plains
18d. Northern
18e. Central
18f. Southern
Costanoan
19a. Saklan (doubtful)
19b. San Francisco
19c. Santa Clara
19d. Santa Cruz
19e. San Juan Bautista (Mutsun)
19f. Monterey (Rumsen)
19g. Soledad

Yokuts
  Dialect groups:
20a. Northern Valley (Chulamni,
      Chauchila, etc.)
20b. Southern Valley (Tachi, Yauelmani,
      etc.)
20c. Northern Hill (chukchansi, etc.)
20d. Kings River (Choinimni, etc.)
20e. Tule-Kaweah (Yaudanchi, etc.)
20f. Poso Creek (Paleuyami)
20g. Buena Vista (Tulamni, etc.)
UTO-AZTEKAN (SHOSHONEAN) FAMILY
Plateau branch
  Mono-Bannock group:
21a. Northern Paiute (Paviotso)
21b. Eastern Mono (Paiute)
21c. Western Mono
  Shoshoni-Comanche group:
21d. Koso (Panamint, Shoshone)
  Ute-Chemehuevi group:
21e. Chemehuevi (Southern Paiute)
21f. Kawaiisu (Tehachapi)
Kern River branch
21g. Tübatulabal (and Bankalachi)
Southern California branch
  Serrano group:
21h. Kitanemuk (Tejon)
21i. Alliklik
21j. Vanyume (Möhineyam)
21k. Serrano
  Gabrielino group:
21l. Fernandeño
21m. Gabrielino
21n. Nicoleño
  Luiseño-Cahuilla group:
21o. Juaneño
21p. Luiseño
21q. Cupeño
21r. Pass Cahuilla
21s. Mountain Cahuilla
21t. Desert Cahuilla

Preface

Californian Indian Nights Entertainments comprises a selection from the myths and tales related at night in the assembly houses and about the campfires of the pre-Caucasian natives of the Golden State.

The stories selected have been adapted from those recorded and published by anthropologists in various publications, to wit: the University of California *Publications in American Archaeology and Ethnology*, the *Journal of American Folk-lore*, and the publications of the American Museum of Natural History. Acknowledgment is here made of the kind permission to utilize these materials, which has been granted by the University of California, the American Museum of Natural History, and the American Folklore Society.

The stories are grouped according to the subject matter with which they deal, and an attempt has been made to have all of the principal regions of California represented so far as possible. Thus, the Redwood empire, the great Sacramento-San Joaquin valley, the Sierra Nevada region, and southern California, are all well represented. The coast region between San Francisco and Los Angeles is poorly represented, because of the early extinction or Mexicanization of the peoples in that region.

The accompanying map shows the location of the various Californian indian groups. It is a reproduction of the 1929 edition of the map issued by the University of California.

The vowels in native words have continental values.

E. W. G.

G. B. H.

University of California, November, 1929.

Introduction

As in many things Californian, the superlative applies to the number of languages spoken within the borders of the state in aboriginal times. One hundred and four languages and dialects were spoken by the aborigines of the state when Caucasians first settled within its boundaries. This vast aggregation of languages within so limited an area is not found anywhere else in the world. There is an approach in two regions, however, to this great linguistic diversity of California. One region is that of the Caucasus mountains, lying between the Black and the Caspian seas, and forming the border country of Europe and Asia, and the other is the vast island of New Guinea in the South Seas – the second largest island in the world.

For many years anthropologists and philologists have recognized twenty-one families of languages in the state of California into which the one hundred and four languages and dialects are classified. Each of the twenty-one families was regarded as coördinate in rank with such great families as Indo-European, to which English, German, Sanskrit, and a host of other languages belong. Certain philologists have united some of the twenty-one linguistic families of California into larger related groups, reducing the total number of major groups to seven. However, these seven major groups are not universally accepted. Whether they are accepted or not, the fact remains that in California there was a perfect welter of diverse languages. Early travelers have remarked on the linguistic change which a few hours of travel brought in California. The accompanying map shows the location of the various Californian groups, and makes clear their linguistic relationships.

Even though the many tribes in California speak a vast number of tongues, stories and myths are frequently shared by contiguous tribes that are utterly different in speech. For instance, the three typical tribes of northwestern California, the Yurok, the Karok, and the Hupa, living on the Klamath and Trinity rivers, share practically all of their myths, even though the languages of these three groups are entirely unrelated, so far as anyone knows. Perhaps this spreading of the tales of one tribe to another may be largely attributed to the presence of bilingual individuals, who were numerous, just as they are along the language borders of Europe, as for instance in Alsace and Lorraine.

Two of the linguistic families, found in California, are also widely represented elsewhere in North America. One of these is the Athapascan family, to which belong Hupa, Kato, and several other languages of California. There are also Athapascan groups in Oregon, and a great mass of Athapascan tribes in the Canadian Northwest, and Alaska. The Apache and Navaho of the Southwest are also Athapascans. In spite of this linguistic relationship of the Californian Athapascans we find that culturally they are like their non-Athapascan neighbors and unlike their linguistic relatives in Alaska and the Southwest. This holds especially in the matter of mythology and folk-tales, although the immediate neighbors of, say, the Hupa, namely the Karok and Yurok, speak languages as different from Hupa as Chinese is from English. Hupa mythology nevertheless closely resembles that of the Yurok and Karok, and is quite different from that of the Navaho and Apache. In other words, the Californian Athapascans have become thoroughly acculturated to the civilization of California, even though still continuing to use their original Athapascan speech. The second great linguistic family extensively represented in California, as well as elsewhere, is the Shoshonean. In California, the Mono, Paiute, Koso, Luiseño, Gabrielino and various other tribes belong to this family. Outside of California such peoples as the Bannock of Wyoming and Idaho, the Shoshoni of Idaho, the Ute of Nevada, Utah, and Colorado, the Hopi of Arizona, and the Comanche of Texas belong to the Shoshonean family. Moreover, the Shoshonean family long ago was shown to be closely related to the Aztekan group of languages in Mexico, so that it is really more correct to speak of the Uto-Aztekan linguistic family than it is to speak of the Shoshonean and Aztekan families. The term Uto has been used in the compound name to take the place of Shoshonean.

Although not recognized by all philologists, it has been asserted that Yurok and Wiyot, two languages of northwestern California, belong to the Algonkin linguistic family, which is so widespread in the great plains and the east. Here also we find that the mythology of the Yurok and the Wiyot is quite like that of their Californian neighbors and that it bears no evidence of close relationship to the mythology of eastern Algonkin tribes.

The list on the key map indicates that several of the

twenty-one linguistic families, which have been long recognized in California, have been united into two major families called Hokan and Penutian. Taking the case of the Hokan family, which is quite scattered, we find again no uniformity in mythology. The mythology of the Karok is like that of their northwestern Californian neighbors, that of the Pomo like that of their central Californian neighbors, that of the Yuman like the mythology of their southern Californian neighbors.

It is evident from the above examples, which we have adduced, that mythology and culture in general may change more rapidly for a people than their language. In other words, people settle in a new environment and proceed to adjust themselves to the mode of life which the people already in the region have established. This adjustment, however, does not necessitate the discarding of their language, which the immigrants have brought with them. Evidently mythology and folklore yield readily to the influence of both physical and social environments, so that stories patterned after those of the new neighboring tribes soon become part of the literature of the immigrant tribe.

The linguistic and dialectic groups of California were, as a rule, not identical with political groups. Thus, in the territory of the central Miwok of the Sierra Nevada region there were some fifty Miwok political units, each one autonomous, though all speaking one dialect. In other words, politically independent communities might have a common language in spite of their autonomy. Tiny communities were often independent to the same degree that the United States is independent of Great Britain. The average village

THE WALKING STICK OF THE GOD YIMANTUWINGYAI, CHILULA
INDIANS

This is a giant redwood which has fallen into the crotch of a neighboring redwood and which is now called the cane of the god. It illustrates how quickly a myth may spring up, because it probably has not been in its present position over a century

THE ROCK WITH DEPRESSIONS

Is said to be the imprint of the hand of the god Yimantuwingyai, Chilula indians

community in central California probably numbered
about one hundred souls. These autonomous units gave
to aboriginal Californian life a separatistic character
quite foreign to our modern Californian organization
into towns, counties, and state.

The languages of California were the medium
through which the myths related in this book
developed. That these languages have had, for many
years, or perhaps even centuries, the form in which we
know them in modern times, is suggested by the fact
that three voyagers of the sixteenth century recorded
words of the Californian languages which they heard
spoken, which are still recognizable today. The voyagers referred to were Alarcon in 1540, Cabrillo in
1542, and Drake in 1579. If their scanty evidence is to
be relied upon, the languages of the three regions which
they visited (the banks of the lower Colorado river,
Santa Barbara, and Sonoma county) have changed very
little in three and a half centuries. It seems doubtful
that we can assume the same stability for all of the
stories and myths which are related in this volume. The
myth episodes apparently travelled much more rapidly
from tribe to tribe than actual words themselves. However, this does not gainsay that many of the myths are
extremely ancient.

The rapidity with which new myths develop is indicated by the myth idea about Yimantuwingyai's walking stick, illustrated in this volume. This is a redwood
tree which has fallen into the crotch of a neighboring
tree. It is likely not to have been in this position for
more than a century, yet the Chilula indians, in whose
territory the tree stands, assert that the fallen tree is the
god's walking stick and that the tree has been in that

position from time immemorial. No doubt many new myth ideas spring up in somewhat similar fashion. Although there was vast linguistic diversity in California, there was not such marked difference in culture or civilization. Tribes speaking quite diverse languages were very similar in culture, just as the various European nations, heterogeneous in language, are nevertheless fairly uniform in civilization. To be sure there are local developments in European civilization, but these do not obscure the broad, underlying foundation of common characters. In California there were three civilizations represented. In northwestern California we find the southernmost extension of the culture of the indians of the north Pacific coast, a civilization typified by extensive wood carving and by social stratification in the castes of nobles, common people, and slaves. These very characters in less elaborate form appeared in the culture of northwestern California.

In like fashion, southern California, south of Point Concepcion and the Tehachapi mountains, was really an extension of the great Southwest culture area, which embraced the southern tier of American and the northern tier of Mexican states.

Only in central California do we find a truly typical Californian civilization, which had developed largely in the heart of California, that is, in the Great valley. This typical central Californian culture extended into the Great Basin, east of the Sierra Nevada, where it was found in less pronounced and less developed form. It will become apparent presently how the mythologies of these three regions – Northwestern, Central, and Southern – differ. The differences in mythologies had their parallels in other phases of the three native civilizations.

THE SOUTHEASTERN POMO VILLAGE OF ELEM ON RATTLESNAKE ISLAND IN THE EASTERN ARM OF CLEAR LAKE, LAKE COUNTY, CALIFORNIA

Showing thatched communal houses each occupied by three or four families

We shall now attempt to picture the fabric of native civilizations, upon which the myths and folk-tales, related in this book, were embroidered.

The only part of California, in which the cultivation of food plants was practiced in ancient times, was the valley of the lower Colorado river and connecting Imperial valley. The crops grown in that region were maize, beans, melons, pumpkins, and gourds, the last not for food but for the making of rattles and canteens. Everywhere else in California no food plants were cultivated, although here and there tobacco was planted. So, with the exception of the people in extreme southeastern California, we are dealing with tribes that gained their subsistence by hunting and fishing and gathering wild vegetable products. By far, the most important vegetable food was the acorn, obtained from various species of oaks. In fact, everywhere that oaks grew in California acorns were utilized by the aborigines. The preparation of the rich and nourishing nut required much labor, for the poisonous tannin had to be leached from it. Seeds, bulbs, and greens in great variety supplemented the staple acorn. In the animal world we find deer, rabbits, and quail furnishing the principal meats. In addition, mollusks and fishes were eaten extensively, and even the insect world was levied upon, for grasshoppers and the chrysalids of certain butterflies were roasted. In northwestern California salmon were particularly important as food. In southeastern California, where oak trees do not grow, the pods of the mesquite tree comprised the most valuable wild food, which supplemented the cultivated crops.

Houses varied. Both dwellings and sweathouses in northwestern California were rectangular in outline and were built of redwood planks. In central California, houses were circular in outline, and ranged from the tiny conical, brush or bark-covered dwelling, a few feet in diameter, to the large semi-subterranean earth-covered assembly house fifty feet in diameter.

Among the Pomo of the Coast range, north of San Francisco, and among the Chumash in the Santa Barbara region, communal thatched houses were erected, each of which was occupied by several families. Among the lower Colorado river indians and in the Imperial valley large rectangular sand-covered houses were built. During the hot summers shades erected in front of these houses were much used.

The sweathouse in central California was small, conical, and earth-covered, to better conserve the heat. It served as a place for sweat baths for the men and was used especially in connection with the treatment of sickness. The sweating was probably efficacious in the treating of rheumatic complaints, but seems to have been a disastrous procedure when applied to some diseases, such as measles. In utilizing the house for sweating three or four men entered it. The fire was built within the house and the men had to lie with their faces close to the ground to prevent being suffocated by the smoke. After they had developed a profuse perspiration they left the house and took a cold plunge in the near-by pool. In northwestern California the sweathouse served not only for the sweating, as in central California, but also as the clubhouse and sleeping quarters of all of the men of each community, for there the men and larger boys did not sleep in the family dwelling, which was occupied at night only by the women and small children.

A HUPA RICH MAN IN GALA DRESS

Consisting of a deer-skin apron, woodpecker scalp head-roll, dentalium shell-money, and eagle-feather ornaments. In his hands he carries a quiver full of arrows and a short stabbing-spear. He is standing on the stone pavement at the entrance to his semi-subterranean sweathouse

Clothing was scanty everywhere in California, and people often went naked. Women's skirts were generally two-piece affairs, comprising a front and a back dress. Men's garments were usually a small apron or breech clout. People normally went barefoot. When traveling rough country, moccasins or sandals might be used, and snow shoes were employed in regions of heavy snowfall.

Implements were made of stone, bone, shell, and wood. Metals were quite unknown. The entire population of California lived in the Stone Age. Only in southern California and the hills bordering the southeastern part of the San Joaquin valley was pottery made. Except among the lower Colorado river indians, Californian pottery was unpainted and makes a sorry impression beside the fine wares of the Southwest.

Weapons comprised the bow and arrow, spear, sling, and club. In southern California a peculiar club of potato-masher form was developed for the special purpose of striking blows on the face. Handy cobblestones were often employed in fighting. Nets, spears, traps, and poison (usually buckeye nuts or soaproot bulbs) were the principal means in taking fish. Nets and snares were also used for birds and at times for deer.

Musical instruments were but poorly developed. The only stringed instrument, used by but a few tribes, was the musical bow. Whistles were of bird bone, flutes of cane or elder wood. Rattles were made of a number of things. In central California split stick rattles and cocoon rattles were employed. The latter was made of large gray cocoons with pebbles placed within. In much of the state a rattle made of deer hoofs was used in connection with the puberty observances for girls.

In southern California rattles were made of gourds and turtle shells.

Most everywhere in California the political unit was a village community, averaging about one hundred individuals. Only on the banks of the lower Colorado river do we find true tribes, which probably averaged two to three thousand individuals each. The three great tribes in that region today are the Mohave, Yuma, and Cocopa.

In northwestern California there were no chiefs. In fact, political organization was lacking. Everywhere else in California there were chiefs. Here and there chiefs were elected, but in many localities they were hereditary, the office usually descending from father to son. Female chiefs were found in parts of central and southern California. The Spanish voyagers, under Cabrillo, encountered such a female dignitary. As a rule in California, chiefs were civil and ceremonial officers, and had nothing to do with military matters. In warfare, command was entrusted to the most experienced warrior, who was usually not the chief. This was true even among the warlike tribes on the banks of the lower Colorado river.

Miwok, Yokuts, and Mono in the San Joaquin valley drainage, and certain of the Shoshonean tribes in southern California were organized on the basis of two great clans or moieties (halves) with the rule that a member of one moiety must always marry a person of the opposite moiety. A child always belonged to his father's moiety. These moieties or clans had certain animals, plants, and natural objects associated with them as totems. There was an indirect connection between this form of social organization and mythology in that both shared the same animals, the animal characters of the myths being the totems of the moieties. For instance, we find that in southern California the two moieties are the Wildcat moiety and the Coyote moiety. The people of the former are jokingly referred to as slow and ponderous in their movements, the latter as quick and tricky in their movements. In the mystic formation of the universe a shadowy sphere was bisected and revealed Wildcat in one half and Coyote in the other.

The lower Colorado river tribes had not merely two clans, but a large number, each of which had a single animal or plant as its totem or emblem. Membership was through the father, as in the moieties. With these tribes there was a curious custom of giving all of the women of one clan the same name, which always had reference to the totem of the clan. Men did not have such clan names.

Disposal of the dead in California was limited to two methods, burial and cremation. The Santa Barbara region and northwestern California were areas in which burial alone seems always to have been practiced. In central California the method of disposal of the dead varied locally. In northeastern California and in southern California, outside of the Santa Barbara region, cremation was the established practice. The custom still prevails along the banks of the lower Colorado river. There the corpse is cremated on a funeral pyre out of doors.

Everywhere some sort of funeral service prevailed. Among the Hupa in northwestern California, the following speech was made at the grave side: "While you were living your time came. May it be well with the people where you used to dwell." Funeral orations were by no means always so brief as this. In southern California the funeral oration often dealt with the destiny of the soul.

Besides the actual funeral services there was in central California and in southern California a sort of memorial or mourning service, held several months or a year after a person's death and sometimes repeated for a number of consecutive years. Marked features of such memorial services for the souls of the dead were the burning of manufactured objects as offerings and the making of images of the dead. These images were invariably destroyed just before dawn on the last night of the ceremony, which often was protracted three or four nights. This type of ceremony had for its purpose the satisfying of the souls of the dead in the other world, through the transmission of the offerings by burning.

After funerary ceremonies perhaps the most important observances in the minds of the natives were those connected with sex, especially puberty. Throughout the state there were special observances for the adolescent girl. At the precise incipiency of womanhood she was usually confined, her diet restricted, and either complete relaxation from work or quite heavy work was imposed upon her, the latter for the magical purpose of making her industrious in later life. A number of other magical concepts entered into the treatment of the girl at this period. For example, she must not scratch her head with her fingers, lest she become bald, therefore a special scratching stick was always provided. This occasion was regarded as especially fraught with importance for the girl as to her future life. In northern California there was the additional idea that

YUKI INDIAN DRESSED TO IMPERSONATE A GOD OR SPIRIT

The god-impersonating ceremonies were held in the semi-subterranean assembly house. This man carries a split-stick clapper-rattle, wears on his head a netting cap full of goose down, across his forehead a brilliant salmon-pink head-band made of flicker feathers and over his shoulders a netting cape with hawk feathers attached

the girl's condition at this time was potentially evil, and that her very glance would blight the oak trees or even the sun itself. Consequently great care was taken that she should not glance at these objects. In one story, that concerning Lady Pelican, the heroine's mishaps are due to her entering the regular daily life of this world too soon after her confinement at puberty.

In central California was found the curious custom of the semi-couvade. The couvade in its full form, as formerly practiced among the Basques in Europe and by certain tribes in Brazil, consisted of the father betaking himself to bed, upon the advent of a child in his family. In central California the husband did not actually go to bed, but he had to remain quietly indoors, and neither hunt, fish, gamble, nor mingle with crowds. It was thought that if he did not follow these injunctions the soul of the new-born infant would be injured and perhaps caused to leave this world. At childbirth women were regarded as unclean, as was also the case each month. Among some tribes there was a special hut erected for the seclusion of women at such times.

For boys puberty ceremonies were but little developed. In northeastern California a boy was whipped with a bow string, sent into the woods alone to hunt, or forced to run races with the lengthening shadows at dusk. In southeastern California the puberty ceremony for boys consisted of piercing the septum of the nose, so that a shell or bone ornament could be worn in it. Without such piercing a boy might not marry. Elsewhere in California boys' puberty rites, if they ever existed, have been subordinated to or incorporated in the cult religions.

In southern California away from the Colorado

river the cult religion centered around the drinking of a decoction of jimsonweed. This contains an alkaloid drug, which produces stupor and visions, the latter of a pleasant character. Through the drinking of this decoction every boy was initiated into manhood and into a secret society. The use of this drug extended to the Yokuts of the San Joaquin valley.

On the banks of the lower Colorado river the cult religion centered around dreaming. The dreaming was of a special character, for the individuals dreamt myths. These they related to audiences. The old men in particular criticized and corrected the portions of the myth which were not dreamt according to the recognized and orthodox style. The use of regalia and dancing were reduced to the vanishing point in this inward looking dream cult. Both the jimsonweed religion and the dream religion in the two parts of southern California were based upon psychic experiences in dreams and visions.

The cult religion in central California was utterly different in its scope. It has been called the god-impersonating cult, for in it the boys and men who had been initiated impersonated gods and spirits. No dream nor vision was prerequisite to participation in this cult. The god-impersonating and dancing took place in the semi-subterranean assembly house. Disguising of the performers, so that they were unrecognizable, as they impersonated deities, was a spectacular feature of this cult. In connection with these indoor ceremonies we find the use of a musical instrument peculiar to central California. This was the foot drum, which was operated by stamping upon it with the bare feet. It comprised half a hollowed log set over a pit. Among some

ILLUSTRATING A NORTHWESTERN CALIFORNIAN BELIEF

By tying the nose and gouging out the eyes of the dead deer it is thought it can neither see nor smell the hunter and thus take cognizance of any possible ceremonial ill-treatment that might befall its body

of the central Californian tribes the initiation of boys consisted of their being slightly cut on the back with a sharp piece of obsidian, wielded by a man dressed to impersonate the widely known god Kuksu. A later initiation, at least among the Pomo, seems to have comprised a mock stabbing and curing of the novice. It should be noted, in passing, that the regalia used in the god-impersonating were extremely sacred and must not be touched by laymen under penalty of becoming ill.

The fourth cult of California was the New Year or renewal cult of northwestern California. As the name implies, the rituals were for the purpose of renewing the world and its products, thus insuring a new and bountiful crop of acorns, or a plentiful run of salmon, or the driving away of sickness from the world, or the causing of warm weather to succeed bitter cold conditions. Although gaudy paraphernalia were worn in the two principal dances of this cult – the white deer skin and jumping dances – these were not sacred and might be touched or worn by anyone. They were simply profane objects of wealth, the treasures of the wealthy men of the tribe. The really sacred thing about the renewal ceremonies was the formula or fiat murmured by the priest, as he sat beside the sacred fire into which he cast incense as an offering to the gods. The god of vegetation was particularly invoked.

A curious belief of the renewal cult was that the souls of slain deer were later reincarnated in other deer. The hunter had to handle venison in a prescribed ritual fashion. The foregoing illustration shows a hunter's precaution against a slain deer smelling or seeing anything ritually wrong at the hunter's house.

Dreams and visions were regarded with far more awe by the indians than by white people. Most indians believed that the soul actually left the body during a dream and went to the places which were seen in the dream. Frequently the indians learned certain songs in dreams; that is, in the dream they heard some one singing. Immediately upon coming out of the dream an indian might wake up and proceed to sing the song which he imagined he had just heard. In that way he made sure that it would not escape his memory. Many songs were obtained, no doubt, in just this manner. This sort of experience occurred particularly with shamans or medicine men, who employed the songs thus obtained as an aid in treating the sick. In his dream a shaman might see some animal or hear the voice of a spirit in other than animal form, which instructed him in the curing of the sick by sucking. It was believed that the creatures encountered in dreamland became the aides and protectors of the dreamer. Knowledge of the other world was also usually credited to dream experiences. Thus, the Kamia indians of Imperial valley said that they knew the souls of the dead went southward to the shore of the gulf of California, because in dreams their souls had visited that region and had seen the rejuvenated souls of the dead.

A sort of waking trance was also sometimes experienced. During such a condition the victim imagined he saw certain monsters or supernatural beings. Among the Miwok, for instance, a man might be hunting, when suddenly there appeared before him the great double-headed rattlesnake Hamaua, of enormous size. This often caused him to faint and while in the swoon he heard a song, which upon reviving he proceeded to sing. Moreover, upon reviving he might find himself bleeding from nose, mouth, and ears. This condition was regarded as a result of the supernatural visitation. A man who underwent such an experience might become a rattlesnake doctor or shaman. As he proceeded homeward after his harrowing experience he perhaps encountered a rattlesnake beside the trail. This he took home with him. Later, he might add other rattlesnakes to his collection. These he used from time to time to demonstrate to the people his ability to handle them. A demonstration of this sort might take place within the ceremonial assembly house. In such a case, the audience sat near the wall of the circular structure, while the rattlesnake shaman released in the center of the house a number of the reptiles with which he toyed. He handled the rattlesnakes in such a way as not to be bitten and at the same time to inspire awe and terror in the audience. This power or deftness of the shaman was regarded as a benefit conferred upon him by the supernatural double-headed rattlesnake during his trance experience. Such a shaman might also be gifted with ability to cure rattlesnake bites.

What we have stated so far with regard to dreams and trances refers wholly to involuntary experiences. Sometimes, however, an indian might deliberately seek a vision or seek contact with the spirit world. For this purpose he went to some lonely mountain top, or to the shore of some unfrequented lake, and attempted to commune with the spirits. This deliberate seeking of contact with the spirit world was rather rare in California, but was common enough in the great plains region, where it was incumbent upon every young man to seek a vision for the sake of the power it would give him in war, in medicine, or in love. In California the seeker after spirit contact, who went to some lonely lake, usually swam in the lake. While thus swimming, the spirit, in the form of a monster, might touch the person's abdomen and cause him to lose consciousness. Upon reviving he found himself upon the shore of the lake, where he was supposed to have been carried by his spirit familiar.

In southern California and in the San Joaquin valley, visions were obtained by boys and young men by still another means. This was the drinking of a decoction of jimsonweed root, already mentioned. This plant is known botanically as *Datura meteloides*. In the narcosis and visions which it produced, the indians said they saw the world. An overdose of the drug was fatal and such fatalities have been recorded from tribes to whom the drug was newly introduced. Among the Colorado river indians jimsonweed was not administered to boys as an initiation, but any individual who wished to, might make a decoction of the leaves of the plant which in this locality is known as *Datura discolor*. A man who wished to have good luck in gambling secretly partook of jimsonweed. Thereafter, when he played peon, the gambling game, he saw the jimsonweed spirit in human form standing behind his opponents—directing him which hand to select in finding the marked bone he sought.

STORY TELLING

The relating of folk-tales and myths seems to be a universal trait of human culture. No modern primitive people is so lowly in culture as not to have an unwritten literature of this sort. In fact, once the investigator begins to delve into the stock of tales which a group possesses, it is truly surprising what a wealth of material is forthcoming. Of course, much depends upon individual informants, for, just as among ourselves, there are both good and bad narrators. A poor narrator is apt to present only the skeleton of the story. A good narrator clothes that skeleton with flesh, and employs the literary devices known to his people. A favorite central Californian device for emphasis in story telling was repetition. For the sake of compactness, repetition has been largely omitted in the central Californian stories in this book.

The narrators among the Californians were usually men, although occasionally a woman raconteur was encountered. Night was the chosen time for relating myths, and winter the favorite season. In fact, there was the belief that harm would befall the story teller if he related myths at any other time. In some groups the story teller was seated; in others, he stood. Among the Kamia indians of Imperial valley he not only stood, but held his hands at his sides and swayed his body sidewise. Sometimes the narrator sang the songs which the various characters were supposed to have sung in the beginning of the world. Singing was thought to be of unusual potency in California, for very often the songs that a person sang were believed to have been received supernaturally during a dream or trance.

In two parts of California, myths were recited not merely as stories, but for magical or ceremonial purposes. Thus, in northwestern California the relating of a myth verbatim, with the proper intonation and inflection of the voice, was believed to be of magical efficacy. For instance, in purifying a person who had handled a corpse and had thereby become contaminated, the priest, who was purifying the person, recited in a low tone the story of the first death in this world, and the subsequent purification of the deceased person's father. Again, on the banks of the lower Colorado river, among the Mohave and Yuma indians, myths were recited publicly in the presence of the old men, who proceeded to criticize the narrator's story. This custom of criticism had a tendency to standardize the various narrators' accounts. The myths among Colorado river tribes, and especially those of creation, were thought to have been dreamed by the respective story tellers. In fact, the Colorado river tribes went so far as to believe that the soul of the narrator was present in the beginning of the world and witnessed the events which the narrator described.

Stories varied much in character, ranging from dignified accounts of the origin of the universe, to petty, childish, or obscene tales. Sometimes a single character in a story might run the gamut from beneficent creator to puerile trickster.

Animal characters were common in Californian tales, and especially so in those of central California. Animal characters served a literary function. They saved the narrator the trouble of describing the attributes of his characters. The use of animal names gave ready-made characterization in the minds of the audience, and made unnecessary elaborate word-pictures describing personalities. It was this extensive use of animal characters that perhaps typified central California most markedly.

In his treatment of the animal characters the narrator gave play to both animal and human attributes. Yet

NORTHERN MIWOK ASSEMBLY HOUSE AT BUENA
VISTA NEAR IONE, AMADOR COUNTY

Exterior and interior view. This structure is built in
the ancient style and is a semi-subterranean earth-
covered affair. It is in such assembly houses that the
Miwok related their myths and tales on winter nights

at no time was there warrant for regarding the animal characters as physically half animal and half human. Everywhere in California the characters portrayed in mythology were spoken of as the "first people," and where these people had animal names the indians stated that they were the first people and that they were later transformed from human beings into the present-day animals. In northwestern California the first people were not given animal names, but were treated throughout as a sort of pre-human race of immortals who disappeared completely from this earth upon the advent of human beings of the present order.

Stories were usually related in some sort of an assembly house or large dwelling. In central California the assembly house was a circular, semi-subterranean, conical-roofed and earth-roofed lodge. Formerly, it was entered through the central smoke hole; nowadays through a side entrance. On the banks of the lower Colorado river stories were related in the large, rectangular, sand-covered dwelling house. As the opposite extreme to this telling of stories before large assemblages may be mentioned the custom of telling the stories to children. An old Pomo informant related how each evening he took his two grandsons on his knees and related myths to them before they went to bed.

Apparently a few European stories or motives have crept into Californian mythology. One such motive was that of a person becoming stuck in pitch; in other words, the tar baby episode. This has been recorded from the Shasta indians. We have mentioned elsewhere the possibility of European influence in the tales which refer to the making of woman from a portion of man.

ORIGIN OF THE WORLD

Beliefs about the origin of the world afford a good example of the diversity of ideas to be found in the three culture areas of California; northwestern, central, and southern. The central Californians entertained the conception of the primeval ocean, followed by true creation, somewhat after the plan of genesis. This idea was also found in parts of southern California.

In northwestern California the concept of creation was wholly lacking. Also there was no belief in a primeval ocean. There the indians believed that the earth was always much as it is now, and that on the earth lived another race of men, who went away across the ocean when the indians came. This race was really immortal and continues to live today, although its members are no longer visible. The chief of this race of immortals was the god Yimantuwingyai, who made the land comfortable for the indians, and found for them the deer, salmon, and other good things to eat. These things, however, were not created, for they were already in existence. How they came into existence was never explained in northwestern stories. In this respect they differed from those of central and southern California. Northwestern California also differed in lacking stories of the destruction of the world by flood or fire.

Throughout southern California there was a vague conception of the earth as a female principle and the sky as a male principle. But with most tribes this idea was subordinated to a true creation story. With the Luiseño indians of San Diego county, however, the true creation idea was lacking, and we find quite a full development of the concept of male and female principles being responsible for all that exists. Even more interesting was the concept of an original void in which the male and female principles developed. These highly abstruse notions were very different from the views of most American indians as to origins, and suggest the ideas of far-away Polynesia. Although we have no proof that such was the case, it is not impossible that a Polynesian canoe may at some time have been wrecked on the southern Californian coast, and its crew introduced this idea which was so unusual for American indians. On the other hand we should not forget that this type of tale concerning the origin of the world, or better still, the universe, fitted in rather closely with the mystic ideas of these southern Californians, with regard to the human soul and other matters of religion.

Among the lower Colorado river tribes flourished the conception of several consecutive creations, each preceding world being destroyed because of the dissatisfaction of the creator with the product of his work. It is here, too, that we find strongly developed the antithetical relations of the creator and his brother, the latter bungling the works of creation which he undertook. In central California his place was taken in some degree by Coyote, who acted as a marplot.

In certain respects the southern Californian creation story which began with a void is the most logical. Other stories of the origin of the world always seem to assume the preexistence of certain things or materials. Thus, in the Diegueño story the creator reached to the west and obtained red ants from which he formed the earth. Other examples of similar inconsistency were to be found frequently in central California, where a number of creatures, in addition to the creator, were already in existence, while the earth was still beneath the waters of the primeval ocean. Moreover, the creator had one or more of these preexisting creatures dive to obtain sand from beneath the ocean. From this sand, sometimes mixed with tobacco, the creator shaped the world. Creation stories, the world over, have illogical elements about them, so that there was nothing peculiar about this among the Californian indians. So, from a logical standpoint, it was the Luiseño of southern California, with their void, who had gone the farthest and had reasoned the origin of matter back to nothingness, and who had realized the significance of maleness and femaleness as creative principles.

Creation stories of the central Californian type are quite common the world over, but conceptions like that of the void among the Luiseño, and of the world having always existed, as among the northwestern Californians, are relatively rare.

Perhaps the most unique conception of the earth was that among the Kato indians of Mendocino county, who pictured the earth as a great dragon, walking down from the north through the primeval ocean. The earth dragon, however, was not the first earth, for that had been destroyed by flood, but was the earth which emerged from the flood. Among the Achomawi of Shasta county a point of special interest was creation by thought. The creator thought of things and instantly they came into existence.

DESTRUCTION OF THE WORLD

The people of northwestern California have neither stories of the destruction and rehabilitation of the world, nor of its creation. Stories about destruction and rehabilitation occurred sporadically in central California and among tribes along the banks of the lower Colorado river. Perhaps the most frequent form of destruction was by flood, sometimes by rain, as among the Kato, or again by overflow of a spring, as among the western Mono indians. The burning of the world was usually thought of as a concomitant of the theft of fire, a thing which people were conceived of as lacking and of which they were in dire need. The destruction of the world by fire suggests somewhat the Norse Ragnarok.

THE ORIGIN OF MAN

In northwestern California, true to form, man was not created any more than were other things. He merely sprang into existence, the signal of his coming being the appearance of smoke on the mountain sides. With the advent of the present race of men there disappeared across the ocean the pre-human race of immortals, which similarly had sprung into existence and which by its acts had pre-determined the character of the indian civilization of northwestern California. In the tales concerning the human race of immortals it is repeatedly said that in such and such a place human beings will behave as did the immortals. The patterning of human culture after that of the immortals did not require a very great stretch of the imagination. But in the stories of the northwestern indians there was one link lacking in the chain of logic. The pre-human race disappeared across the ocean before the present human race appeared. This inconsistency, however, did not deter the indian story teller from saying that modern human culture was patterned after that of the immor-

tals. By the three principal tribes of northwestern
California the immortals were known by three different
names: Woghe among the Yurok, Ihkareya among the
Karok, and Kihunai among the Hupa.

Contrasting with the northwestern Californian indian idea of no creation and no original birth, was the
Luiseño idea of human beings as the offspring of the
earth mother and sky father. More correctly it seems
not to have been the actual physical body of man which
was brought forth by the earth mother, but the human
spirit or soul. The Luiseño and neighboring tribes, like
the Gabrielino and Juaneño, all of Shoshonean speech,
seem to have been especially interested in the matter of
the origin and destiny of the human soul. Much of
their religion focussed upon this matter. Thus, we find
that they conducted religious ceremonies in which the
human soul was typified and the immortality of the
soul was indicated by symbolic acts, such as stepping
into and out of a pit; the pit, of course, representing the
grave, and the stepping out of the pit representing the
escape of the human soul.

In much of central California and on the banks of
the lower Colorado river flourished the puerile conception of men and women being made from sticks or
from clay. The common story in central California
was that Coyote, or some other deity, hid sticks in a
house over night, and in the morning they arose as men
and women. On the banks of the lower Colorado river
men and women were made from clay, but owing
to the fact that they disobeyed the creator they were
destroyed and a new lot of people created. Thus, it is
very clear that we have three distinct conceptions of
man's origin in California, just as we have three corre-

sponding conceptions as to the origin of the world. To recapitulate, the three are: (1) No creation, but springing into existence, in northwestern California; (2) birth from the earth mother, in the western part of southern California; and (3) true creation, in much of the remainder of California, especially in central California, where the creator who made man was sometimes conceived of as human, at other times as animal, or as at least bearing an animal name.

Here and there we encounter the concept of woman being made from a part of man, such as his rib. Each instance of this sort is open to the suspicion that it may be due to Biblical influence, which after all has been operating in parts of California for a century and a half.

A very distinctive feature of human anatomy, which received a certain amount of attention in central California, was the hand. When man was being made, Lizard and Coyote debated as to whether or not man should have a hand like Coyote or a hand like Lizard. Needless to say, Lizard won the argument.

THE DESTINY OF THE SOUL

It is probably true to state that there was no tribe in California without some belief in the existence of the soul after the death of the body. The conception of the land of the dead varied. In the northwestern part of the state the idea of an underworld was found together with that of a sky world, to both of which the souls of the dead went. In the San Joaquin valley, among the Yokuts, there was the belief in an island of the dead. In southern California, especially among the Shoshonean peoples, the milky way and the stars were the abode of the dead. On the banks of the lower Colorado river and in Imperial valley the land of the dead was placed on the shores of the Gulf of California, and the souls of the dead were believed to be rejuvenated there in human form. Following repeated death and rejuvenation they ultimately became owls or beetles, and their existence in human form was completely ended.

On the banks of the lower Colorado river, too, existed the concept, unusual in America, of soul theft. It was thought that the souls of deceased relatives came from the land of the departed and abducted the soul, or one of the souls, of a living person. Living persons were often conceived of as possessing more than one soul. Abduction of the soul caused illness. This non-material concept of the cause of illness was markedly different from the theory of disease which prevailed elsewhere in California, where it was thought that sickness was caused by the injection of foreign substances into the body. In southern California, hair was regarded as particularly sacred and symbolical of the human soul, and ropes of human hair were used in connection with the sacred sand-painting and the moral lecture which was read to boys. The ropes running from the center of the sand-painting to the four cardinal directions were said to tie the soul to this world. The lectures laid particular stress upon the life conduct, especially in relation to elderly people.

Among the Luiseño the abode of the souls of the dead was in the sky, where they traveled over the milky way, or became stars. At funerals, it was customary to blow upward and to motion upward with the hands, with the idea of aiding the soul of the dead person to

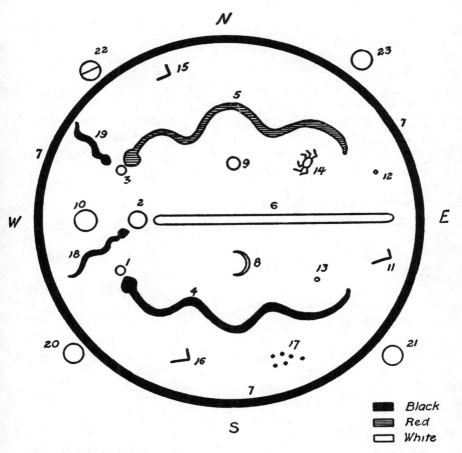

NORTHERN DIEGUEÑO GROUND PAINTING, REPRESENTING THE UNIVERSE

Made in seed meal and sands of various colors and is used in connection with the lecture to boys following the jimsonweed initiation

Explanation: Ground painting made by Antonio Maces and Jo Waters, old men at Mesa Grande, San Diego county. 1, 2, 3, Jimsonweed mortar and pestle; 4, 5, Rattlesnake; 6, Milky way; 7, World's edge; 8, New moon; 9, Full moon; 10, Sun; 11, Coyote; 12, Buzzard star; 13, Crow; 14, Black spider; 15, Wolf; 16, Mountain-sheep, Orion; 17, Pleiades; 18, Black snake; 19, Gopher snake; 20-23, Mountains

rise to its new home where it was apparently conceived of as dwelling forever. The ability of the soul of the deceased to go to its new abode was largely dependent upon leading a good life in this world. Part of the initiation of boys into the secret society of the jimson-weed cult comprised a lecture or sermon delivered over a ground-painting or dry-painting, which was made on the ground with different color sands and meals. The illustration of the Diegueño form of ground-painting, represents the various celestial bodies and various terrestrial creatures. These various things were supposed to be the agents and watchers of an all pervading god, who, among the Luiseño, was called Chungichnish. These objects were referred to usually by sacred double names. Thus the bear and the panther were called bear-panther. A certain mythical creature, whose name cannot be translated into English, was referred to by the native name of Apmikat. This word might perhaps be best translated as "breaker."

The following is a literal translation of the lecture or counsel which was given to boys over the ground-painting.

"See these, these are alive, this is bear panther; these are going to catch you if you are not good and do not respect your elder relations and grown up people. And if you do not believe, these are going to kill you; but if you do believe, everybody is going to see your goodness and you then will kill bear panther. And you will gain fame and be praised and your name will be heard everywhere.

"See this, this is the raven, who will shoot you with bow and arrow, if you do not put out your winnowing basket. Hearken, do not be a dissembler, do not be heedless, do not eat food of overnight (i.e., do not secretly eat food left after the last meal of the day). Also you will not get angry when you eat, nor must you be angry with your elder relations.

"The earth hears you, the sky and wood-mountain see you. If you will believe this you will grow old. And you will see your sons and daughters, and you will counsel them in this manner, when you reach your old age. And if when hunting you should kill a hare or rabbit or deer, and an old man should ask you for it, you will hand it to him at once. Do not be angry when you give it, and do not throw it to him. And when he goes home he will praise you, and you will kill many and you will be able to shoot straight with the bow.

"This is a black rattlesnake, this is going to bite you. Do not eat venison, do not eat jackrabbit, do not eat chia, do not shout in presence of old people. And if old people arrive at your house, you will welcome them at once. And if you have no food to give them, you will tell them so politely. And if you have, then you will give them some at once, also water. And when they arrive at their house, they will praise your goodness, and you will have a good name. And if a rattlesnake should bite you far off in the field, you will be able to arrive at your house. But if you should be wicked and heedless, you will not arrive; right there you will die in the field. And people will say that you are heedless, and that for that reason the rattlesnake bit you.

"See this, this is a black spider, this is going to bite you. Do not steal food of overnight, do not eat hurriedly when you are hungry. Also when you rise in the early morning you will bathe in the water, and you will always be active, and you will win when you run races.

And the people will praise you, and you will shout, and will throw away food. And you will not eat much, or your body is going to be heavy, and you will get tired when you run races, and you will sting your foot with nettle.

"See this, this (apmikat) is alive, this is going to break you, this is going to lame you, this is going to cause you to have boils on your body, this is going to make you blind, this is going to give you consumptive cough. In the early morning you will bathe, and if illness comes it will pass you by, also blood (i.e., blood vomiting sickness).

"When you die your spirit will rise to the sky and people will blow (three times) and will make rise your spirit. And everywhere it will be heard that you have died. And you will drink bitter medicine, and will vomit and your inside will be clean, and illness will pass you by, and you will grow old, if you heed this speech. This is what the people of long ago used to talk, that they used to counsel their sons and daughters. In this manner you will counsel your sons and daughters.

"This is the breaker, this is going to kill you. Heed this speech and you will grow old. And they will say of you: 'He grew old because he heeded what he was told.' And if you die at some future time you will be spoken of as those of the sky, like the stars. Those it is said were people, who went to the sky and escaped death. And like those will rise your soul (towish). In this manner you will counsel your sons and daughters, should you have any. Pay heed to this speech, that was spoken by the people of long ago.

"See this, this is going to splinter you, this is going

to give notice what you do, this is going to see you, this is going to know if you have bad thoughts. And if you marry, you will not approach your wife when she is menstruating. The rattlesnake is going to bite you, the stick is going to splinter you, consumption is going to catch you, the earth and sky are going to see if you do anything bad. Listen to this speech and you will grow up and become old. And you will think well of your elder relations and they will say of you: 'He is good, whose son is he?' In this manner you will counsel your sons and daughters.

"And if a bear or panther will wish to catch you, they will not overtake you. And if a rattlesnake or black spider should bite you, you will not die. But if you are heedless and a despiser, right there you will die. And your spirit (heart) will not rise to the north, or your soul (towish) to the sky."

Most everywhere in California the stories imply, or in some cases directly state, that man was to be immortal. Through one cause or another the boon of immortality was denied him. In northwestern California people died because two children of the culture hero were put into the ground alive and remained there until they died. If their father had been successful in his plea for their resurrection, then mankind would likewise have been immortal. But unfortunately, the culture hero's wives insisted that the children must remain in the ground and must not come to life. In central California somewhat similar stories were told of the argument following the death of the first person. Sometimes Coyote, sometimes Meadowlark, objected to resurrection and insisted that the dead person should remain dead, thus establishing the precedent for all mankind. In southern California the first indication that death would be the lot of all mortals in this world was the death of the god Wiyot. However, he was resurrected as the new moon, demonstrating that the soul did not die. Following his death others met with the same fate and thus it became apparent that no one could escape death. The concept of the dying god, as it is called, was widespread in southern California and extended all of the way from the Pacific ocean to the Colorado river.

Among the Shasta indians of northern California it was said that the soul left the body before death and there were certain seers who professed to be able to see the footsteps of departing souls in the atmosphere. These suddenly appeared in the air, and then melted away. By the shape of the footstep the seer could tell who it was that might be dying at a distance.

There was little implication anywhere in California that the sort of life one led on earth was instrumental in determining the destiny of his soul. In southern California boys were told that if they did not behave properly their souls would not rise to the sky at death. In northwestern California, among the Hupa, there was a differentiation of soul destiny. The souls of shamans and singers of the dances went to a pleasant abode, the world of the Kihunai, in the sky. The souls of all others went to a dismal underworld, where there were no fires, where it was foggy and cold, and where food must be eaten uncooked. In the San Joaquin valley the Yokuts told of an island of the dead, which periodically became over-crowded, so that it was necessary to transform some of the human souls into fish.

Among the Maidu, the soul was believed to repair to

an abode in the sky. There were local variations as to how this abode was reached. One of the most interesting told of the soul ascending with the rising sun until the meridian was reached, thence proceeding to the milky way, which was the pathway to the other world.

In the Sacramento valley the Maidu believed that when a person died his soul left the body through the mouth, and was like wind. The souls of good people traveled to the other world by a well-lighted trail, plainly marked; whereas those who had been wicked journeyed in darkness, over a trail so indistinct that they had to crawl on hands and knees painfully feeling for the road. All, whether good or bad, eventually reach the same place, which was called Heaven valley, a beautiful region where lived the Creator and where there was an abundance of food, all of which was easy to secure. The Creator had a tiny basket full of delicious food, from which all who wished might eat; and although a hundred might eat from it, yet it ever remained full. The ghosts of bad people, although they went also to Heaven valley, proceeded to a less desirable portion, where all was not so charming and comfortable.

Stories of visits to the land of the dead have been recorded, and suggest the Orpheus and Eurydice story of the ancient Greeks. Among the Hupa it was said that there was a trail which led straight west, down into the underworld. On this trail, however, was a red house in which a family lived. When a person was in a trance or a faint his spirit traveled only to this house, for the spirit that went beyond never returned to this world. From this house there led two trails. One went to the underworld, the other to the world in the sky. The road to the underworld led to a river Styx, which was guarded on both sides by water gods. There were split canoes for the spirits of the dead to cross the river. A story was related how a man followed his beloved dead wife's soul down this trail, put the gods to sleep with powerful tobacco, crossed the river, and brought back his wife. She was unhappy, however, and could not enjoy the world of mortals again, so he had to allow her to return to the underworld.

Ghost stories were not very common in California. Ghosts were visualized as appearing like human beings, but as being gray in color. The sight of a ghost was usually sufficient to cause illness. In both central and southern California it was customary for people to burn offerings for the benefit of the souls of deceased members of their families. These offerings were presented to the dead in connection with the mourning ceremonies. It was thought that the offerings would make the dead satisfied, so they would not desire to return to the homes of the living. On the banks of the lower Colorado river there was entertained the idea that if the dead were satisfied they would not return to steal the souls of the living.

THE QUEST OF FIRE

As with peoples in different parts of the world, many of the Californian tribes conceived of a time when mankind was without fire; or, at least, when a certain tribe was without fire. The Californian stories usually related the dissatisfaction of the people over eating uncooked food and over the discomfort of cold. Then some enterprising member of the community discovered that people in another locality had fire. Certain individuals were delegated to steal the fire. The attempt was invariably successful, although there might be a disastrous sequel to the theft, as for example, the burning of the world. The character who played the part of Prometheus varied from tribe to tribe. With the Sierra Nevada Miwok it was the flute player, Mouse, who lulled the fire owners to sleep, concealed some coals in his flutes, and escaped. With other tribes, Coyote played the leading role.

An interesting sequel to the Miwok tale of the Theft of Fire was the explanation of the diversity of language. Those who sat close to the new fire spoke Miwok, those who sat far away in the cold, could not speak correctly, and in consequence the Mono language was spoken by them. This attitude in the Miwok story was quite typical of California. Each little group regarded itself as speaking correctly, and all other peoples as speaking brokenly.

THE ORIGIN OF THE SUN AND MOON

Practically all the Californian peoples who discussed the origin of the sun and moon regarded them as something which was obtained or made only after man himself had come into existence on earth. They did not think of the sun as a primeval object, existing from the very beginning. In central California the presence of the sun was usually accounted for by a theft story, the sun being possessed by people far off and being stolen from them for the benefit of the tribe relating the story. In southern California the sun was made usually from clay or spittle. The Californians were in no sense sun worshippers, and that luminary played a very unimportant part in their religious beliefs. Moreover, they gave very little attention to the yearly movements of the sun, and most tribes did not take special note of the time of the solstices, although these could easily enough have been determined by simple observations. By some tribes in central California, such as the Yuki, the sun was conceived of as a deity who was the patron of doctors who cured rattlesnake bites.

A person bitten by a snake looked at the sun, as did also the doctor. If it appeared milky to the latter, he knew his patient would recover, and proceeded to cure him. He began by threatening or abusing the sun; after which he painted wavy lines, apparently representative of rattlesnakes, on a flat stone, warmed the wounded part with hot ashes, laid the stone on it for a time, and then began to suck. The belief was that a tiny living rattlesnake was in the body, which the sucking drew towards the shaman's mouth and then into it. However, just before the small snake left its victim to enter the shaman's mouth it died, so that it was only a dead snake that the shaman produced.

Of even less importance than the sun in California was the moon. The Maidu had a tale about the restriction of the movements of the two luminaries to night and day. In northwestern California there was the interesting belief that the waning of the moon was due to its being eaten by Lizard in the sky. The story of greatest human interest about the moon was that told by the Luiseño of southern California, who regarded the moon as a symbol of resurrection. They declared that it was the incarnation of the god, Wiyot, the first individual to suffer death upon this earth, also the first to undergo resurrection, hence setting the example for all mankind.

Some attention was paid to the moon in connection

with the crude calendars of the Californian tribes. In northwestern California the months were numbered. In central California they were named for the condition of the vegetation or the actions of animals. In these two regions usually twelve month names were employed, but, inasmuch as there were more than twelve moons in the year, the application of the month names varied in the course of a few years, and no careful account was kept of the exact number of moons. For instance, in central California the condition of the vegetation was really the prime factor in naming a given month. As a good illustration of this we give the following calendar of twelve moons, which comprised a year, among the central Pomo indians:

Stalpikelda. Leaves turning yellow and dropping. November.
Sachauda. Cold winds; sometimes snow.
Bashelamataula. Buckeye nuts getting ripe enough to eat.
Kadamchidoda. Roots and flowers commence growing.
Chidodapuk. Flowers blooming.
Umchachichda. Seeds and other plant foods ripening.
Putichda. Edible bulbs (wild potatoes) ripening.
Bakaichichda. Manzanita berries ripening.
Luchichda. Acorns appearing on the oaks.
Sachluyiauda. Soaproot dug for fish poisoning.
Kalemkaiyoi. Building fire at foot of big tree to fell it and obtain wood.
Kasida. Beginning of cold weather.

In southern California prevailed the curious custom of employing only six month names. These were used twice during the year, thus a month in the dry season and a month in the wet season both bore the same name. This type of naming the moons or months was also found in the Pueblo region of the Southwest.

A Shasta story, which we present, really deals with the months rather than the physical moon.

COYOTE TALES

The character Coyote was by far the most popular and widely known in California, and the stories about him were legion. Even in the mythology of northwestern California, which had a minimum of animal stories, Coyote, nevertheless, appeared. Usually he was portrayed as a male and his rôles ranged from creator to that of a mean and gluttonous trickster. Among the northwestern Maidu, Coyote opposed the plan of immortality for men. He was the first to suffer for this through the death of his own son. Sometimes Coyote's deceit was turned to good account, as among the southern Maidu, where one tale related how he destroyed a cannibal by trickery. Among the Patwin, Coyote was a real benefactor, for he extinguished the world conflagration, renewed water, and created people from sticks. In his rôle of trickster he often was bested. A not unusual tale dealt with Coyote and his mother-in-law. When it is recalled that many central Californian tribes had a taboo against speech between son-in-law and mother-in-law, it will be realized that stories dealing with the mother-in-law gave opportunity for comical situations. It is perhaps in connection with the varied play upon Coyote's character that the Californian's ability as a story teller appeared at its best. Just why this character appealed so to the Californians and to other indians in western North America is difficult to say. His position in Californian mythology was very much like that of the Raven in north Pacific coast mythology.

THE GRIZZLY BEAR

The grizzly bear, the most impressive large mammal of California, one would imagine should have appealed to the indians much more as a character for tales than Coyote. However, this seems not to have been the case, although there was built up around the grizzly bear a belief analogous to that of werewolves, in Europe. In central and southern California it was thought that certain men were bear doctors and had the power to turn into grizzly bears at will, and in such form were more terrible than true grizzlies. As recently as 1920 an individual who was reputed to have this ability was still living near Banning in southern California. It was thought that the human being who had taken the form of a bear was invulnerable. He might to all appearances die as a bear, but would come to life again as a man.

Among the Pomo indians there was a special variant of the idea about the bear doctor. He was thought not to transform himself into a bear, but merely to wear a bear skin as a disguise, and to carry a bone dagger with which his victims were murdered. Although model suits of this bear doctor's disguise have been made for museums, ethnologists have yet to find a single person who was reputed to have been such a "doctor" among the Pomo.

MONSTERS

Much of central and southern Californian mythology and folk-tales bore a close resemblance to those of Europe, and a number of tales in this book are of this type. We have incorporated, for example, tales about giants who ate human beings, about rolling heads, and about various evil beings.

The rolling head concept was quite common in central California. A person was believed to eat himself, all but his head, and then to roll about in search of human victims whom he devoured.

A very common conception of the Mono and the Paiute indians of the Great Basin of Nevada and Utah, was that of the water sprite, which was termed in English a "water baby." It was visualized as human in form and with long flowing tresses. If one of these sprites were offended, it would cause a flood, in an attempt to drown the offending person. Perhaps related to the water baby was the mermaid of the Yosemite region.

As in Europe, some of the central Californians peopled the woods with tiny dwarfs. Thus, the Maidu and Miwok told of such creatures meddling with sleeping people, but doing no serious harm. Then, too, the Miwok sometimes saw tiny fairies dancing in hollow trees. One such fairy, which was represented in Miwok dances, was called Tula.

In southern California, in the vicinity of Mount San Jacinto, was to be seen at times the phenomenon called the electric fire ball, or ball lightning. All of the tribes in that region regarded this phenomenon as an evil spirit, who made his home in a huge rock in a canyon on Mount San Jacinto; in fact, in the very canyon which is denoted on the maps by the name of the spirit, to wit, Takwish canyon. This evil being was said to carry away people to his house, where he feasted upon them. A wealth of stories developed around this demon.

Many a spring and stream was regarded with awe by the indians as being the habitation of some dragon or other monster. Among the Pomo a frequent means of appeasing such monsters was to cast offerings of arrowpoints into the water. Certain illnesses among the Pomo were believed to be caused by a woman seeing one of these monsters when she went to fetch water from a spring. The treatment for such illness suggests modern psycho-analytic methods. The doctor secretly made an image of the monster, which he suddenly exposed to the sick woman. She exhibited the same symptoms of fright, as upon seeing the original monster in the spring. Then the doctor showed her that she was only looking at an image, and assured her that what she saw in the spring was equally harmless.

Perhaps related to the casting of arrowpoints into springs as offerings, was the northwestern Californian custom of shooting or casting arrows into a tree as offerings to a local spirit. Sticks and stones were also deposited as offerings at rest places both by northwestern and central Californians. It was thought that such offerings would end fatigue and danger on a journey.

Somewhat resembling the animal stories of Europe were the numerous animal stories of California. However, this should be remembered about the latter: these animal people were thought of as having existed as human beings once and as then having been transformed into their present animal forms. In other words, they were the "first people." Some of these stories had an explanatory element, telling how the crow became black, how the chipmunk got his stripes, or how the robin got his red breast.

SKYLAND

Californian mythology had very little to say about the sky, though various groups regarded parts of the sky as the abode of the souls of the departed. Among

NORTHERN DIEGUEÑO WHIRLING DANCER
In paint and eagle-feather skirt

AN ARROW TREE, HUMBOLDT COUNTY
Arrows were shot into certain trees as offerings to local
spirits

the Miwok there was the concept of a skyland, which was reached through an opening near the horizon. This entrance had a door, which was continually opening and closing, so that passage through was a risky matter. Then, too, this skyland might be reached by going straight upward, as illustrated by the story "Kidnapped in Skyland."

The sky was the abode of the thunders, who were thought of as persons who once lived on earth, but who went to the sky and became thunders. These thunder stories were particularly typical of central California.

STAR STORIES

Star stories were rare in northwestern and central California, but common enough in southern California. They accounted for certain constellations. The usual explanation of these constellations was that the individual stars were once people who lived on earth. The Pleiades were perhaps the favorite constellation about which stories were told. Among the lower Colorado river tribes, where agriculture was practiced by the indians, who grew crops of maize, beans, and pumpkins, planting time was determined by the position of certain stars. This coincided with the high stage of the river, which inundated its banks and made agriculture possible in a region which was well nigh rainless. Here there was a duplication of the primitive conditions of the Nile valley of six millennia ago.

The southern Californian indians saw in the sky such things as archers, and various animals, much as we imagine that we see the various animal and human forms in the constellations. Among the Shoshonean tribes of southern California the stars had a special sacred significance, for they were regarded as the souls of the dead and the milky way was the pathway over which souls traveled. In fact, the whole religion of southern California was much more concerned with the human soul and its destiny than were the religions of central and northwestern California.

ADVENTURE STORIES

A number of stories concerned the adventures of human and animal characters. Such stories usually involved more or less travel. However, travel stories *par excellence* were to be found especially among the lower Colorado river tribes. The Mohave, for instance, had travel stories, the telling of which took three or four nights. These stories reveled in infinite and burdensome detail as to locality and as to what the traveler thought and did at each place. The region covered, however, by such travel stories was usually very limited, and did not involve travelling over the whole world. These peculiar travel stories seem to have been one of the special developments of lower Colorado river culture, just as dreaming was one of the special developments of religion in that region.

MIGRATION TALES

In northwestern and central California there were no migration tales. The various tribes sprang into existence, or were created, in the localities in which they lived. This absence of migration tales correlated with one characteristic of life: in former times men rarely got more than twenty miles away from home in any direction, so that attachment to a given locality became exceedingly strong during one's lifetime. Indeed, each person desired to be buried where he was born. In southern California we find quite a different situation. There there were migration stories similar to those of the Southwest. These tales usually began with the origin of the world and the creation of mankind. Then they settled down to recounting the wanderings of mankind from the far north. Ultimately the movements of the particular tribe that told the story were related. Thus, the Luiseño, for example, came from the far north and finally arrived at Temecula in Riverside county. There the god Wiyot died and various other events of importance to mankind took place. Temecula was regarded by the Luiseño as their most sacred place and as the center of the world. Beyond the actual habitat of the tribe concerned, such migration tales were not to be regarded as dealing with definitely known places. They were rather a manifestation of a widespread type of myth episode and were not to be regarded as historical.

The Origin of the World and of Man

The Origin of the World and of Man

THE EARTH DRAGON

[As told by the Kato indians of Mendocino county]

Before this world was formed there was another world. The sky of that world was made of sandstone rock. Two gods, Thunder and Nagaicho, looked at the old sky because it was being shaken by thunder. "The rock is old," they said. "We will fix it. We will stretch it above, far to the east." Then they stretched the sandstone rock of the sky, walking on the sky as they did so. Under each of the four corners of the sky they set up a great rock to hold it. Then they made the different things which would make the world pleasant for people to live in. In the south they made flowers. In the east they made a large opening so that the clouds could come through. In the west they made an opening so that the fog from the ocean could come through. To make clouds they built a fire. They said that the clouds would keep people, who were to be made later, from having headaches because of too much sunshine.

Then they made a man out of earth. They put grass inside him to form his stomach. Another bundle of grass they put in the figure to make man's heart. For his liver they used a round piece of clay, and the same for his kidneys. For his wind pipe they used a reed. Then they prepared blood for man by mixing red stone, which they pulverized, with water. After making the various parts of man the two gods took one of his legs, split it and made a woman of it. Then they made the sun to travel by day and the moon to travel by night. But the creations of the two gods were not to endure, for flood waters came. Every day it rained, every night it rained. All the people slept. The sky fell. The land was not. For a very great distance there was no land. The waters of the oceans came together. Animals of all kinds drowned. The waters completely joined everywhere. There was no land or mountains or rocks, but only water. Trees and grass were not. There were no fish, or land animals, or birds. Human beings and animals alike had been washed away. The wind did not then blow through the portals of the world, nor was there snow, nor frost, nor rain. It did not thunder nor did it lighten. Since there were no trees to be struck, it did not thunder. There were neither clouds nor fog, nor was there a sun. It was very dark.

Then it was that this earth with its great, long horns got up and walked down this way from the north. As it walked along through the deep places the water rose to its shoulders. When it came up into shallower places, it looked up. There is a ridge in the north upon which the waves break. When it came to the middle of the world, in the east under the rising of the sun it looked up again. There where it looked up will be a large land near to the coast. Far away to the south it continued looking up. It walked under the ground.

Having come from the north it traveled far south and lay down. Nagaicho, standing on earth's head, had been carried to the south. Where earth lay down Nagaicho placed its head as it should be and spread gray clay between its eyes and on each horn. Upon the clay he placed a layer of reeds and then another layer of clay. In this he placed upright blue grass, brush and trees.

"I have finished," he said. "Let there be mountain peaks here on its head. Let the waves of the sea break against them."

The mountains became and brush sprang up on them. The small stones he had placed on its head became large. Its head was buried from sight.

Now people appeared. These people all had animal names, and later, when indians came to live on this earth, these "first people" were changed into the animals which bear their names. Seal, Sea Lion, and Grizzly Bear built a dance house. One woman was named Whale. She was fat and that is why there are so many stout indian women today.

The god Nagaicho caused different sea foods to grow in the water so that the people would have things to eat. He caused the seaweed to grow, and also the abalones and mussels, and many other things. Then he made salt from ocean foam. He made the water of the ocean rise up in waves and said that the ocean should always behave in that way. He said that old whales would float ashore, so that the people might have them to eat.

He made redwoods and other trees grow on the tail of the great dragon, which lay to the north. He made creeks by dragging his foot through the earth so that people would have good fresh water to drink. He traveled all over the earth making things so that this earth would be a comfortable place for men. He made a great many oak trees, so that the people would have plenty of acorns to eat.

After he had finished making everything, he and his

dog went walking all over the earth to see how all of the new things looked.

Finally when they arrived at their starting point he said to his dog: "We are close to home, my dog. Now we shall go back north and stay there."

So he left this world where people live and now lives in the north.

HOW THE EARTH WAS MADE
[As told by the Yuki indians of Mendocino county]

In the beginning everything was water. On the water, in a fleck of foam, a down feather circled. From this came a voice and singing. This was the creator Taiko-mol who was to make the world. His name means He-who-goes-alone. With him was the god Coyote. After a time the god who was in the feather came to look like a man. All the time that he was taking on the appearance of a man he was singing. Then he made a basket from parts of his own body. From this basket he made the earth which he fastened and strengthened with pine pitch. Then he traveled over it four times from north to south with Coyote hanging to his body. Next he fastened the four corners of the earth and made the sky from the skins of four whales. Then he made people by laying sticks of wood in a house overnight. In the morning these sticks had turned into people.

Taikomol wanted people to live forever, but Coyote's son died and was buried. The god offered to bring him to life, but Coyote said that the dead should remain dead and for that reason people do not come to life again after they die.

ABOVE-OLD-MAN DESTROYS HIS FIRST WORLD
[As told by the Wiyot indians of Humboldt county]

Above-Old-Man made some people a long, long time ago. They were the very first people created, but they were not right. They could not talk right and they were all furry.

"How am I going to get rid of them?" thought Above-Old-Man.

Then he decided what he would do. He would cause water to cover all the earth.

Condor knew what was going to happen, but no one else did. He and his sister wove a large, deep, basket. It took a long time to finish, but at last it was ready. Then when the flood came they both got into this basket and closed it tight. They felt it being tossed around by the waves. When it at last ceased to move, Condor decided it had anchored, so he and his sister pushed open the cover and stepped out. The flood had subsided, and all around was the land, but there were no people.

Condor began to fly about over the land. He came upon many birds – pigeons, doves, and others. When he discovered the tracks of a raccoon, he called to his sister. But she did not like him to call her sister. He puzzled about this for awhile and then decided: "When I again address her I shall speak to her as 'my wife.' "

So he did, and she laughed, for that was what she had wanted.

They married and soon a baby was born. From then on people kept on being born. These people were good, talked well, and looked handsome. Above-Old-Man was content. He knew they were good people, and he liked them.

This was the world after the flood.

THE BEGINNING OF THE WORLD
[As told by the Achomawi indians of Shasta county]

In the very beginning all was water. The sky, as far as one could see, was clear. It did not have any stars, or clouds, or anything in it. Then one day a cloud formed in it, grew lumpy, and turned into Coyote. Next a fog arose, grew lumpy, and became Silver Fox. They became persons.

They both looked down at the world, which was entirely of water, and thought how nice it would be to have a canoe, and a canoe appeared on the water.

"Let's stay here. Let's make it our home," they said to one another.

They floated about for many years and the canoe became old and mossy. They grew very weary of this.

"Do go and lie down," said Silver Fox to Coyote, one day.

While Coyote slept Silver Fox combed his hair and saved the combings. When there were many of these combings Silver Fox rolled them in his hands, stretched them out, and flattened them between his hands. Then he laid them upon the water and spread them out until they covered all the surface of the water. This became the earth. Silver Fox looked at it and thought of trees, of shrubs, and rocks, and they were there.

Then he cried to Coyote: "Wake up! We are going to sink."

Coyote woke and looked up. He saw the trees and

heard crickets. "Where are we," he asked; "What place is this we have come to?"

"I don't know," Silver Fox replied. "We are just here. We floated up to the shore." But Silver Fox was not telling the truth, for he knew, since he it was who had made the world. He did not want Coyote to know that the world was his creation.

"What shall we do?" Silver Fox asked. "Here is solid ground. I am going ashore, and am going to live here."

So they landed and built a house and lived in it.

After a time they thought about making people. They made little sticks of serviceberry, and thrust them all about in the ceiling of the house. By and by all became people of different sorts, with the names of birds, animals, and fishes.

THE BEGINNING OF THE WORLD
[As told by the northwestern Maidu of Butte county]

All the earth was covered with water, and everything was dark in the beginning. There was no sun, no moon, no stars. Then one day a raft appeared, floating on the water. In it was Turtle. Down from the sky a rope of feathers came and dangled near the bow of the raft, and then a being, who shone like the sun, descended. He was Earth Initiate. When he reached the end of the rope he tied it to the bow of the raft, and stepped in. His face was covered, so that Turtle was not able to see it. In fact, no one has ever seen his face uncovered. Earth Initiate sat down and for a long time said nothing.

"Where do you come from?" Turtle asked at last.

"I come from above," Earth Initiate said.

Then Turtle asked: "Brother, can you not make for me some good dry land, so that I may sometimes come up out of the water?"

Earth Initiate did not answer at once, and Turtle asked, "Are there going to be any people in the world?"

After thinking for awhile, Earth Initiate said, "Yes."

"How long before you are going to make people?" Turtle asked.

"I don't know," Earth Initiate answered. "You want to have some dry land: well, how am I going to get any earth to make it of?"

"If you will tie a stone about my left arm I will dive for some," Turtle answered.

So Earth Initiate did as Turtle asked. Reaching around he took the end of a rope from somewhere and tied it to Turtle.

"If the rope is not long enough I will jerk it once, and then you must haul me up; if it is long enough I will give two jerks and then you must pull me quickly, as I shall have all the earth that I can carry."

Turtle was gone for six years, and when he came up he was covered with green slime, he had been down so long. He returned with only a very little earth under his nails. The rest had all washed away.

Earth Initiate scraped the earth out from under Turtle's nails, and put it in the palm of his hand and rolled it about until it was round and about the size of a small pebble. This he laid on the stern of the raft, and went away and left it. Three times he returned to look at it, and the third time found that it had grown very large. The fourth time he looked at it it was as big as the world, the raft was on ground, and all around were mountains.

When Turtle knew the raft was on ground, he said: "I cannot stay in the dark all the time. Can't you make a light so that I can see?"

"Let's get out of the raft, and then we will see what we can do," Earth Initiate replied.

As they got out Earth Initiate said: "Look that way, to the east! I am going to tell my sister to come up."

Then it began to grow light, and day began to break, and the sun came up.

"Which way is the sun going to travel?" Turtle asked.

"I will tell her to go this way, and go down there," Earth Initiate answered.

After the sun went down it grew very dark.

"I will tell my brother to come up," said Earth Initiate.

Then the moon rose.

"How do you like it?" Earth Initiate asked Turtle.

"It is very good," Turtle answered. "Is that all you are going to do for us?"

"No, I am going to do more yet."

Then he called the stars each by name and they came out.

Then he made a tree, which had twelve different kinds of acorns growing on it. [This tree grew at Durham, Butte county.] For two days they sat under this tree, and then both set off to see the world which Earth Initiate had made. Turtle was not able to keep up with Earth Initiate. All he could see of him was a ball of fire flashing about under the ground and the water. When they returned from going around the world Earth Initiate called the birds from the air, and made the trees, and then the animals.

Some time after this he said: "I am going to make people."

So he took dark red earth and mixed it with water, and made two figures, one a man and one a woman. He lay down and placed the man on his right side and the woman on his left. Thus he lay all afternoon and night. Early in the morning the woman began to tickle him in the side. Earth Initiate kept very, very still and did not laugh. Soon after he got up, he put a piece of wood into the ground, and fire burst out.

The two people Earth Initiate made were very white. Their eyes were pink, their hair was black, their teeth shone brightly, and they were very handsome. He named the man Kuksu, and the woman Morning Star Woman.

When Coyote saw the two people Earth Initiate had made he asked him how he had made them. Earth Initiate told him, and Coyote said to himself: "That is not difficult. I will do it myself."

He did just as Earth Initiate had told him. But when early in the morning the woman poked him in the ribs just as she had done to Earth Initiate, he could not help laughing. Because Coyote laughed the people were glass-eyed. When Earth Initiate saw these glass-eyed people he said: "I told you not to laugh."

Coyote declared he had not laughed, but he told a lie. This was the first lie told in the world.

After a while a great many people were made. Earth Initiate wanted to have everything comfortable and easy for the people, so that none of them should have to work.

Earth Initiate did not come as often to the world as he had in the beginning. He only came to see Kuksu in the night. One night he said to him: "Tomorrow morning you must go to the little lake near here. Take all the people with you. I will make you a very old man before you get to the lake."

So in the morning Kuksu called all the people together and started off to the lake. By the time he reached it he had become a very old man, just as Earth Initiate had predicted. He fell into the lake, and sank out of sight. Then the ground began to shake, the waves overflowed, and there was a great roaring under the water, like thunder. Soon Kuksu appeared from the water, and most marvelous of all, he was young again!

Earth Initiate appeared and said to the people: "If you do as I tell you, everything will be well. When any of you grow old, so old that you cannot walk, come to this lake. You must then go down into the water, as you have seen Kuksu do, and you will come out young again."

Then Earth Initiate left and went above. For a long time everything was fine in the world. Food was easy to get. The women simply set out baskets at night, and in the morning they found them full of food, lukewarm and all ready to eat.

But one day Coyote came along. When he learned how easily the people were living, he said: "That is no way to do. I can show you something better. We will have a mourning ceremony and burn property."

The people did not know what he meant.

"I will show you," Coyote said. "It is better to burn property for the dead, for then the widows can be free."

So Coyote took all the baskets and things that the people had, hung them up on poles, and made everything ready. Then he said, "At this time you must always have games." So he fixed the month during which these games were to be played. He told them to start the games with a foot race; so everyone got ready to run. Only Kuksu did not attend. He sat in his house alone, and was sad, for he knew that death was going to come into the world.

Rattlesnake came to Kuksu and asked: "What shall we do? Everything is spoilt."

Kuksu did not answer, so Rattlesnake said: "Well, I will do what I think is best." He then went out along the course that the racers were to run, and hid himself in a hole. Soon the racers came into sight, and among them was Coyote's son. As he passed the spot where Rattlesnake had hidden himself, Rattlesnake raised his head and bit the boy in the ankle. In a minute the boy was dead.

All the spectators saw Coyote's son fall, and they laughed and said to Coyote, "Your son has fallen down and is so ashamed that he does not dare to get up."

But Coyote said, "No, that is not it. He is dead."

This was the first death.

The people however did not understand and picked the boy up and brought him to Coyote. Coyote began to cry and everyone did the same. These were the first tears.

Coyote took his son's body and carried it to the lake, of which Earth Initiate had told them, and threw the body in. But there was no noise, and nothing happened, and the body drifted about for four days on the surface. On the fifth day Coyote went to Kuksu with four sacks of beads. He begged him to restore his son to life. Kuksu did not answer. For five days Coyote begged.

Then Kuksu came out of his house, bringing all his beads and bearskins, and called all the people to come and watch him. He laid the body of Coyote's son on the skin and wrapped it carefully. Then he dug a grave and put the body into it and covered it.

"From now on this is the way you must do," he told the people. "This is the way you must do until the world shall be made over."

Quite a while after this a great change came over the world. It happened one night. The people were burning offerings for the dead, when suddenly everybody began to speak a different language; only each man and wife spoke the same language. Earth Initiate came to Kuksu in the night and told him about it, and instructed him what to do. When morning came Kuksu, who was able to speak all the languages, called the people together, taught them how to cook and to hunt, gave them all their laws, and set the time for all their dances and festivals. Then he sent the warriors to the north, the singers to the west, the fluteplayers to the east, and the dancers to the south. He told them that that was where they were to live.

These people, who spoke different languages and were sent to all different parts of the world by Kuksu, were the forefathers of the different indian tribes.

THE MAKING AND DESTROYING OF THE WORLD
[As told by the western Mono indians of Madera county]

In the very beginning of things, all the world was under the water. Prairie Falcon and Crow sat on a log which stuck up above the water, and surveyed all around them. They decided that there would have to be a world above the water. So Prairie Falcon went to Duck.

"What number did you dream?" he asked him.

"Two," replied Duck.

Upon hearing this Prairie Falcon gave him the number three and told Duck to dream again, for three days this time, and while in this state of dreaming to dive into the water and bring up some sand from the bottom. He warned him that he had only three days in which to do this, for he could only remain beneath the water while dreaming.

Duck dived to get the sand, but before he reached the bottom the allotted three days expired. He awoke from his dream to find himself far down under the water. He died as a consequence, and his body floated to the surface. When Prairie Falcon saw his floating body he brought him back to life.

"What is the matter?" he asked.

"I came out of my dream and so died beneath the water," Duck replied.

Prairie Falcon next sent Coot down below to obtain earth for the making of the new world. He allowed Coot two days to do this in, but Coot also failed to reach the earth under the water before his two days expired. He, too, died and his body floated on top of the water. Prairie Falcon brought him back to life, also.

Then Prairie Falcon tried once more. This time he sent Grebe down for earth, allowing him four days in which to obtain the earth. Grebe succeeded in reaching the bottom. There he picked up sand in both of his hands and started to return to the surface, where Prairie Falcon and Crow were awaiting him. But as he was

returning he passed out of his dream state, died, and
floated to the surface. Prairie Falcon brought him back
to life, as he had the other messengers.

"Did you secure any sand?" he asked.

"Yes," Grebe replied.

"What have you done with it?" Prairie Falcon inquired, for he could see no sand in Grebe's hands.

"It all slipped from my hands when I died," Grebe
explained.

Prairie Falcon and Crow both laughed at him and
said that they did not believe him. But Grebe insisted
that he had obtained the sand. So Prairie Falcon and
Crow examined his hands. They found sand under the
finger nails of both. They took the sand and threw it
in every direction. That is what made the world.

But things did not go entirely right after the earth
was made. Condor had made a spring and was going
about capturing people and bringing them to his spring.
There he beheaded them and allowed their blood to
run into the water. Every time he left his house he returned with a victim, whom he took to the spring and
beheaded. Soon the spring became full of blood.

Condor then built a fire under the spring, so that the
blood would boil over the rim and flood out his neighbors. Even after this he was not satisfied, and next he
dug a ditch from his spring to Ground Squirrel's house.
Thereby he flooded Ground Squirrel's home. Three or
four of the Ground Squirrels escaped from the house,
and Condor caught one and carried him to the spring
for slaughter. Before he chopped off Ground Squirrel's
head, however, he laid him beside the spring and
stooped to take a drink, for he was thirsty.

Condor's daughter approached and spoke to Ground Squirrel.

"If you do not kill him, he is going to flood out everybody," she said.

So Ground Squirrel cut off Condor's head, as he drank. But when he did so the water which Condor had drunk ran forth in every direction, killing all the inhabitants of the world. And thus did the flood destroy the world which Prairie Falcon and Crow had made.

THE WORLD BEFORE THE COMING OF THE INDIANS
[As told by the southern Miwok indians of Mariposa county]

There were six different races which lived in this world before the indians. The first people were just like the present indians. For a long time these people lived on the earth, and then one day there appeared in the north a great cannibal giant, Uwulin. He commenced to eat the people in the north, and from there he traveled all over the world, with a hunting sack on his back, in which he placed the people he ate. This hunting sack was so large that it would hold all the people of a village at once. The cannibal giant had hands so large that he could, at a single grasp, hold a person between each two of his fingers. Soon he had eaten nearly everyone.

There was one peculiar thing about Uwulin. He could not be killed unless shot through the heart; and his heart, instead of being in the place our hearts are, was in a tiny spot in his heel. This, however, the people did not know, or they would have long since tried to kill him. Finally, the few people still left in the world got together and discussed what to do to rid themselves of this cannibal giant before he killed them, too.

At last Fly found Uwulin asleep. He began at the giant's head, traveled over every part of his body, biting him. The giant slept on, unaware of Fly's bites. It was not until Fly reached Uwulin's heel and bit there, that the giant jerked his foot and kicked. Then Fly knew that he had found the place where the giant's heart lay. Fly returned and told the people of his discovery.

The people held a council and discussed how they might kill Uwulin. Finally they decided to make a great many large bone awls and to place them all along the trail over which Uwulin traveled. They placed them in such a manner that Uwulin could not walk without their sticking into his feet. Finally one of them pierced his heart and he died immediately.

His death took place near the present town of Coulterville, and it is said that a few years ago a man found there the petrified bones of Uwulin. They were of immense size, especially the head. The man died within a few days after digging out these bones.

The second race of people who lived on this earth were the Bird people. A spirit by the name of Yelelkin stole most of these people, and the remainder left because the world was overrun by big black ants. Thus came to an end the second race of people.

The third race of people who came to live on the earth were half animal and half human. The chiefs of these people lived in Bower cave, which is on the old Coulterville road to the Yosemite valley. Later these people turned into our present birds and animals. Among these people was Raven who was a great hunter. Each time he returned from a hunt he brought a great quantity of food for the chiefs. Later, when the people turned into the birds and animals whose names they bore, the great quantity of food stored in the cave hardened and turned into stalactites and stalagmites, which can be seen to this day in the cave.

However, before Raven became such a good hunter he had trouble. His body was originally pure white, and when he went hunting the deer saw him before he could get near enough to shoot them. So he smeared charcoal paint all over his body to make himself harder to see. That is why today ravens are black in color.

The fourth people who lived on the earth were, like the third people, also birds and animals. Skunk, who was chief of this fourth race of people, was an overbearing, mean man. He made his people hunt deer for him, and when brought home, dried and stored the meat. He ate what he wanted, but fed his people, the hunters included, only on acorn mush and other such common foods.

In order that his hunters might kill a great many deer for him, Skunk directed them to hunt in this way. He stationed them all behind trees. Then he went to where many deer were and discharged his horrible scent at them. The deer fled in the direction of the hidden hunters, who shot at them, one at a time, as they came running.

After a time, however, the hunters began to grumble at Skunk's treatment of them. They could see no reason why they should always hunt for Skunk's benefit and never receive even a taste of the meat. Finally, they decided that the only way to escape oppression was to kill the tyrant. But they could not kill him above ground because of the terrible odor which he was sure to emit. So Badger dug a hole in which to kill Skunk, and the people filled it with red hot coals and then covered it over with soft earth, so that Skunk would not know it was a hole. They invited Skunk to dance that night. All sat around and watched him, and as he danced they praised him loudly. He danced more and more violently and they praised him more loudly. Gradually, however, Skunk sank deeper and deeper into the soft earth covering the pit, and finally he sank out of sight. The people ran to the hole immediately and covered it with large stones. Skunk began to shoot his scent in a vain endeavor to escape. This caused mountains to rise up out of the level surface of the earth, but did not help him any, and he finally died in the pit. The people then all had a great feast on his stored meat. When they were through they all turned into the animals whose names they bore.

How the fifth race of people came to be and what happened to them is a mystery to this day.

The sixth race of people came about in a very different way. The earth then was covered by water. One day Coyote informed Frog that he had decided to make foods and people.

"This is all very well, to create all kinds of things, but what good will that do while there is nothing but water here," Frog answered. "How can your people live without land?"

So Coyote went to Duck, and then to Watersnake, and to each he said: "Dive and see if you cannot find some dirt."

They each dived but failed to return with sand. Frog then dived and returned with two handfuls of sand. This sand Coyote scattered all around, and thus made land upon which his people could live. Then he planted many kinds of food, such as pine nuts and acorns. Coyote next gathered about him six wise men. To them he said: "I have decided to make some good people in this country."

They asked him what kind he intended to make.

"I do not know exactly, but I am sure I can make them in some way," he answered. "You see, we have all kinds of food so we must make some people to use it."

The wise men suggested that Coyote create people at once, and he agreed to do so.

He said, "Do you see my foot? Do you think people could use a foot like that?"

"No," said Waterdog, "look at mine."

"Well, yours is the same as mine," said Coyote, "both are round."

Then Lizard spoke up.

"Your feet are certainly too round. How can people pick up all kinds of foods if they have feet like yours? Now look at my foot. It has five toes, so that I can pick up anything, shoot the bow and arrow, and do many useful things easily."

"You are right." said Coyote. "Yours is the proper kind. I shall make people and place them all over the world."

"All right," agreed Lizard, "You know how to make them, so go ahead."

Thus did Coyote create the people with hands and feet like Lizard's. Then Coyote turned to Frog.

"You like the water. You shall continue to live in the water hereafter," he told him.

Thus he spoke to each of the animal people and told

what form each should have and where each should live in the future, since the world was now to be peopled by human beings.

THE MAKING OF HUMAN BEINGS
[As told by the Lake Miwok indians of Lake county]

Hawk Chief was always complaining. This time he wanted people.

"Grandfather, why aren't there people?" he said. "There ought to be people."

Coyote got very angry at this.

"All right," he said. "All right. Now you have spoiled it. There will be people, but we will have to go away."

So Coyote made people. He shut himself in his house while he carved people of wood. He used all kinds of wood: white oak, redwood, fir, pine, black oak, sugar-pine, buckeye, maple, live-oak. He carved them like sticks and stuck them in the ground all around the house. Then he sang and danced the rest of the night.

"In the morning you will be people," was what he sang.

Next morning they were people.

Then Coyote proceeded to give them names.

"You are Bluejay, and you, you are Deer, and you, you are Dog," he said, as he named everyone of the sticks.

But these people did not know how to talk. So Coyote made a big dance. He made these people dance all night, while he was singing.

"Tomorrow, you will talk," he said.

When they awoke the next morning, the people were all talking.

"The fleas were terrible last night," they were saying
to each other. "Those fleas nearly finished us."

Then Coyote spoke: "Good morning."

But the people were still talking about the fleas.
Coyote was vexed at this.

"Yes, that's all right," he said, "but listen to me, now.
I am going away. My grandson doesn't like it here, so
I am going away. We are going away."

Then he said to his wife, Frog Old Woman: "Come
on, old lady, gather your things and your baskets; let's
go."

Then he spoke again to the human people.

"When you die, you are to come to my land. Beyond
the ocean I shall be. None but the dead people are to
come to my land. Not living people. Dead people
only. After four days they are to come to my land, the
dead people."

Then he went away with Frog Old Woman, Hawk
Chief, and all his people.

THE BEGINNING OF THE WORLD
[As told by the Costanoan indians of Monterey county]

When this world was finished Eagle, Humming
Bird, and Coyote were standing on top of Pico Blanco,
a high mountain in Monterey county. The world was
being flooded and when the water rose to their feet
Eagle carried Humming Bird and Coyote and flew
away to a still higher mountain. There the three stood
until the water went down. Then Eagle sent Coyote
down the mountain to see if the world was dry.

Coyote came back and said: "The whole world is
dry."

Eagle said, "Go and look in the river. See what there is there."

Coyote did so and came back, saying, "There is a beautiful girl."

Eagle then said, "She will be your wife, in order that people may be raised again."

Eagle gave Coyote a trowel of abalone shell and a stick to dig with.

Coyote married the girl. Coyote's children went out over the world and became the forefathers of the different indian tribes.

Then Coyote gave people the bow and arrows with which to kill rabbits. He told them they were to make mush and bread from acorns and that they were to eat seaweeds and abalones and mussels.

Coyote thought he knew more than anyone else, but Humming Bird really knew more. Coyote wanted to kill him because he was jealous of him. He caught Humming Bird and mashed him completely. Then he went away.

Humming Bird however came to life and flew after Coyote, crying in mockery at him: "I am dead."

Then Coyote wondered how he could really kill Humming Bird. Some others told Coyote that he would have to swallow him to kill him. But once Humming Bird was inside of Coyote he scratched him so that Coyote had to let him out.

In the ocean lived various kinds of animals. Coyote told his wife about most of these. But one animal which is very frightful he did not tell her about. When she was at the beach once, this animal came out of the water and she was so frightened that she fell over dead. Then Coyote took her on his back, carried her away, and built a fire and laid her beside it. He sang and danced and jumped. When he had done this three times she came to life again.

Although Coyote did many good things for people he was at times rather stingy and mean, even with his own children. He caught salmon and put them in the ashes to roast. He wished to eat them all himself, so he told his children that there were no salmon there, only ashes. Once in a while he reached into the ashes, took a piece and ate it. Then his children cried out that he was eating fire and would be burned. When they wanted to take some he would not let them. He said: "You will be burned."

THE BEGINNING OF THE WORLD
[As told by the Juaneño and Luiseño indians of Orange, Riverside, and San Diego counties]

There was in the very beginning nothing whatever. There was no sky, no earth, no water, but just empty space. In this empty space there became two clouds. One was called Vacant and the other was called Empty. They were brother and sister.

This brother and sister kept changing into different forms, until finally the brother became Sky and the sister became Earth.

Then the sister said what she, Earth, would be like. "I shall stretch out and become large," she said. "I shall shake, making earthquakes. I shall roll around and around."

Then her brother, Sky, told what he would be like. "I shall rise up and become the sky and arch over everything," he said. "I shall cause men to die and take their souls up to heaven."

Then the sky brother and the earth sister became the father and mother of everything which is to be found in this world. Most of the different things were born as twins. The things that were born were hair and the things made of hair, baskets, throwing-sticks for killing rabbits, water and mud, red paint which came from springs, and green paint which came from ponds, the rose and the blackberry, the mountains and rocks, the turkey vulture, the black oak tree, the brake fern, the black and red rattlesnakes, the raven and the bear, the spirit of man, and many other things.

All of these things were really people which were born. They were the "first people," and later they were changed into the different things named.

These "first people" were born far away in the north where it was dark. In the darkness they traveled southward, until they came to a place where there was a high mountain which stopped them. However, they found a way to pass by the mountain through a very narrow canyon. Finally, they arrived at Lake Elsinore and at last at Temecula in Riverside county. Temecula became the center of the world.

It was only after these "first people" arrived at Temecula that the sun was made and there was light. The "first people" raised the sun up into the sky with a net.

With the "first people" was a very good man or god, named Wiyot, who became the ruler of the people.

After a time Frog, who was a wicked person, became jealous of Wiyot, who was a good person and who did everything he could to make people happy and comfortable. She bewitched Wiyot and made him very ill. Wiyot's mother, the Earth, made a remedy to cure

Wiyot of the illness, but Coyote, who was always a meddlesome fellow, spilt the medicine and as a result Wiyot died. He told people, however, that he would return again, even though he died.

After he was dead the people decided to burn his body but they were afraid that Coyote would meddle again and spoil the funeral, so they tried to burn his body while Coyote was away. All had burned except Wiyot's heart when Coyote appeared. He cried and said he wanted to see his brother Wiyot. He jumped right over the heads of the people at the funeral, ran up to the fire where Wiyot's heart was burning, seized it, and ran away with it.

Then Kingbird said that Wiyot would come to life again in the form of the moon, and surely enough people saw the new moon in the west for the first time.

Wiyot was the first person to die in this world. The other people then began to realize that they too would have to die. Eagle traveled in every direction, north, east, south, and west, to try to escape death, but he found death everywhere, so he gave up his attempt to escape and after a time he too died.

Deer, in the same way, tried to escape death but found it was useless, and that people would kill him with arrows.

Up to this time everybody had spoken one language and all could understand one another. But Night, who was really the sky brother whom we first spoke of, decided that it would be best to divide up the people and give them different languages and send them away to different parts of the world to live. So Night arranged this at Temecula and people went to all parts of the world to live.

After a while there was born at Los Alamitos in Orange county a man or god named Chungichnish who told the people that he had come from the sky to be their ruler. He instructed the people how to make the sacred ceremonies and instituted the order of jimson-weed initiates. He told them of the rules of conduct which they must obey.

He, too, became sick and said that when he died he would go up to the stars, from which he would watch people, and that if people disobeyed his rules he would punish them by making them sick or sending starvation, or by having a bear or rattlesnake or mountain lion bite the bad persons.

Every indian boy and girl is told about Chungichnish and his rules as to how they should behave and as to how they would be punished if they did not behave. Among the commandments is that telling all young people to be respectful and kind and polite to their elders.

The god Chungichnish promised people that if they obeyed his commandments, at death they would rise to the sky to live with him among the stars.

THE BEGINNING OF THE WORLD
[As told by the Diegueño indians of San Diego county]

In the beginning there was no land. There was nothing but salt water, the great primeval ocean. Under this water lived two brothers who always kept their eyes closed because of the salt water which would blind them if they opened their eyes.

After a time the oldest brother, Chaipakomat, rose to the surface of the water and looked around. He saw nothing but water. Soon the younger brother came up, but on the way he opened his eyes and the salt water blinded him, so that when he did reach the surface he could see nothing and therefore returned to the deep. The older brother decided that there should be something in the world beside water, so he first made little red ants. He made so many of them that they filled the water very thickly with their bodies. This made land. Then Chaipakomat caused certain birds with flat bills to come into being, but because there was no sun or light these birds got lost. So Chaipakomat took three kinds of clay, red, yellow, and black, and made a round flat object. He threw this up against the sky and it stuck there. Soon it began to give a dim light. Today we call this the moon. But Chaipakomat was not satisfied, for the light was poor. So he took some more clay and made another round flat object and tossed that up against the other side of the sky. It also stuck there and sent forth a very bright light. We call this the sun.

After this Chaipakomat decided to make people. He took a piece of light-colored clay, rolled it, and split it part way, and made a man of it. Then he took a rib from the man and made a woman.

After Chaipakomat had made the world and the people in it, he went away and turned into a snake. He lived on an island in the ocean, far to the west. Chaipakomat had swallowed all learning, just before he became a snake. Singing, dancing, basket-making, all were inside of him. A huge monster guarded him and saw that no one got any of the learning away from him. He would swallow all who came near.

Now the people wanted to have a ceremony, but they could not dance or make speeches. So they decided to send to the snake and ask him to give them the dances. One man changed himself into a bubble and went to the island where the snake was. But the monster saw him and swallowed him. The bubble-man, when he found himself down inside the monster, went in all directions seeking a way out. Then he thought of a flint, and he had it. With this he cut a hole through the monster and got out. He walked up to the house in which the snake lived and went in.

"Who are you who comes into my house?" the snake asked.

"It is I, uncle," the man answered.

"Tell me what you want," said the snake.

"I come from the people," answered the man. "They are trying to make a ceremony there, but they do not know how to sing or dance."

"All right," said the snake, "I will come and teach them. You go ahead and I will come slowly."

So the man went back, the serpent following him.

The people prepared a dance house ready for the ceremony. When the snake arrived he went into the dance house. First he put his head in; then he began slowly pulling his length in after him. There seemed no end to him. His body was tremendously long, and he kept coiling himself around and around as he pulled in more of his body. The people became afraid as they watched, so they threw fire on top of the house and burned him up. As he burned all the learning inside of him came flying out, and scattered all around. Thus the people received the learning they wanted.

THE BEGINNING OF THE WORLD
[As told by the Yuma indians of Imperial county]

In the beginning water was everywhere. Two men lived at the bottom of the water. One day one of these men came up to the surface of the water. As he sailed up he kept his eyes closed. His name was Kwikumat. As the second man came up out of the water, however, he opened his eyes, and thus became blinded by the water entering his eyes. Kwikumat called him Blind-Old-Man.

Kwikumat was not pleased with the world of water as he gazed around. So he thrust his finger into the water and stirred, reciting:

> I am stirring it around, I am stirring it around.
> It will be dry land, it will be dry land.

The place where he was stirring became dry land.

"Ah, it is too small," said Blind-Old-Man. "There will not be room enough for the people."

"Be patient, you old fool!" said Kwikumat.

Blind-Old-Man seated himself on the ground and took up some mud with which he started to shape human forms.

"What are you trying to make?" asked Kwikumat.

"People," said Blind-Old-Man.

"You must first watch me, and see how I make them," said Kwikumat.

Blind-Old-Man said nothing. He was angry.

Kwikumat then busied himself with making the moon and a star. This he did by placing spittle on the forefinger of his right hand, and then he rubbed his finger on the eastern sky until he made a round shiny place. At the same time he made just one star.

"This moon shall not stand still. It shall move toward the west," Kwikumat said.

"But it will go into the water, and how will it get out again?" asked Blind-Old-Man.

"I shall turn the sky so that the moon will move

along the northern horizon, and thus reach the east again," answered Kwikumat.

"I do not believe that," said Blind-Old-Man, as he continued working on his mud people.

Kwikumat, who had intended also to make people for his world, was afraid that Blind-Old-Man would beat him. He sat down and took up some mud. He made a Yuma man and woman, a Diegueño man and woman, a Cocopa man and woman, and a Maricopa man and woman.

Blind-Old-Man soon showed Kwikumat his people, but Kwikumat said they were not right, for Blind-Old-Man's people had no toes or fingers. They had feet and hands like ducks. Blind-Old-Man argued with Kwikumat, and finally Kwikumat kicked the figures, which Blind-Old-Man had made, into the water. Blind-Old Man flew into a rage and jumped into the water after them. He made a great whirlpool as he sank down. Out of this whirlpool a foul wind came, bringing all kinds of sickness to the world. Kwikumat tried to stop the wind from escaping out of the whirlpool by placing his foot upon the pool, but some of the foul wind still escaped, so that is why there is sickness in the world.

Kwikumat then went to the different kinds of people he had created, and told them where they were to live and also taught them how to speak. He told the Yuma woman that she was to marry the Yuma man.

The woman, however, said: "I want a good-looking husband. I don't want that Yuma man. The Cocopa man is handsomer."

"Don't marry the Cocopa man for you and he are destined to dwell in different places," Kwikumat answered.

The woman did not believe Kwikumat. She went away and sulked.

Then Blind-Old-Man arose out of the water and went to her. "Do not believe what Kwikumat tells you. He can do nothing for you. But if you believe in me you will have many possessions and eat six meals each day."

Kwikumat knew that the woman did not believe him. "You did not believe what I told you," he said. "Therefore I shall destroy you and all the other people."

Kwikumat faced the north and talked rapidly four times, and then it rained for four days, covering the world with water. He transformed the people, excepting the Yuma man, into animals.

Kwikumat then decided to try making a new world. He had his son make the sun and stars. Then he, himself, made more people. His son caused plants to grow, gave people their seeds to eat, and showed people how to cultivate plants. The Yuma man made various animals such as Coyote, Raven, and Mountain-lion. These animals behaved so badly that Kwikumat became angry and sent a second flood, which rose upwards until it touched Raven's tail. Then the water went down as he did not wish to drown Raven.

Again Kwikumat decided to make a new world. Now children were made. Kwikumat also made Rattlesnake, who bit the Yuma man, causing him to die from the bite. But Kwikumat brought him back to life. In punishment Kwikumat threw Rattlesnake into the northern ocean where he is believed to dwell today as a great sea monster. The people whom Kwikumat created did not like one another and because of this

Kwikumat destroyed them by fire. A few good people were saved by Kwikumat's son who buried them in snow. Then Kwikumat sent another flood. The waves were so high that they washed the earth into mountains as we now see them.

But there came a time when Kwikumat offended his daughter, Frog, and she caused him to die by witchcraft. While dying he urged his son to complete his work.

After Kwikumat was dead they burned his body, but as it was burning Coyote stole his heart which he ate.

Meantime, Rattlesnake in the northern ocean, had grown to an enormous size. Kwikumat's son invited him to come to help cure a sick man. When he came, however, Kwikumat's son killed him. The snake's blood became gold, his spit became silver, his head became gravel, and his body became a bulwark around the earth.

Kwikumat's son then made the Colorado river flow forth, by thrusting a spear into the ground. With the spear he also cut its channel. Then he took the people to a mountain. Here they built him a house. In the house he instructed the people in religion, and he gave to the different clans the names of animals and plants. Then he sent the various tribes to their present places to live.

The Yuma man became sick and died near the present town of Yuma in Arizona. His body was then burned on a mountain. Kwikumat's son sank into the earth where he remained four days. Then he came out and turned himself into four different kinds of eagles. He has been in these forms ever since. So at last, after making the earth four different times, the creators were

satisfied and left the earth in the condition we have it
today.

HOW THE WORLD WAS MADE COMFORTABLE FOR PEOPLE

[As told by the Hupa indians of Humboldt county]

In northwestern California the god who made the
nice things in this world for people is known as Yimantuwingyai, which in English means He-who-is-lost-to
us-across-the-ocean. He first appeared in a place on
the Klamath river. When he came into existence there
was a ringing noise throughout the world like the striking of a large bell. Just before he appeared in this
world smoke had settled on the mountain sides and
rotten pieces of wood fell from the sky. Where they
fell there was fire. After he appeared there grew everywhere in the world a race of people who lived there
until the indians appeared, when they went away across
the ocean never to be seen again. These people were
immortals who did not die. Some of these people were
bad and the god who came first did not like them. One
of these bad people had all of the deer in his keeping.
He kept them inside a mountain through the side of
which was a door. The god, not liking this, set out to
find a way by which he could let the deer out of the
mountain so that everybody could have venison to eat.

He went to the house of the stingy person who kept
all of the deer.

He said: "I am hungry for fresh deer meat."

The owner of the deer went to kill a deer to give the
god some of it to eat. The god secretly watched him to
see what he did. He saw the man open a door in the
side of the mountain where the deer were kept. The

god ran back to the house before the man returned. He put his quiver, in which his arrows were kept, on the roof of the house; then he went inside. When the man brought the deer the god made an excuse to go out. He said: "I am going out to take a swim before I eat the deer meat."

As he passed out he took down his quiver from the roof. In it had grown a plant called wild ginger, of which the deer are very fond. He now went secretly to the door behind which the deer were kept. He opened the door and laid the ginger on the ground. The deer came out and smelt the ginger and scattered all over the country. In that way it became possible for everybody to have deer meat to eat, instead of only the one stingy person who had them all in the beginning.

Then the god thought that it would be a nice thing if he could have some sort of fish for people to eat everywhere. A woman who lived across the ocean toward the north had all of the salmon in the world, in a pond there. Although she ate plenty of fish herself she would not allow the fish out of the pond for fear other people might catch them. The god arrived at this selfish woman's house. He was very polite to her and called her his niece. She gave him fresh salmon for the evening meal. The next day the god, having spent the night there, told the woman he would like some eels to eat. When she went to catch them he followed to spy upon her. Having found out what he wished to know he hurried back before the woman arrived with the eels. She cooked the eels and called to him to come and eat.

After he had remained at the woman's house for two nights he again felt hungry for salmon. When she went for them he followed to see what she would do. He saw the fishing platforms projecting out over the water and many fish nets near-by. He also saw the nets for catching surf fish.

The next day he said he was hungry for surf fish. He watched her get them as he had done before. Then she cooked them for him between two sticks.

Now that the god had found out what to do to get the various kinds of fish for people to eat, he made a flute of wood. He told the flute that when he went out it should play, so that the woman would think he was still there.

He looked around to see the best place for digging a ditch from the pond to the ocean, so as to let the salmon and other fishes out. He dug a ditch with a sharp stick. When the ditch was finished the water rushed out, carrying the fish with it, so that they were able to swim to all parts of the world. The stingy old woman ran along after her salmon, telling them to come back, but they went swimming away just the same. Every year this old woman follows the salmon up the Klamath river and the Trinity river, when they swim up those rivers to lay their eggs. They speak of her as Salmon's grandmother. She is believed to appear in the form of a small yellow-breasted bird, a fly-catcher.

The god traveled over the world making things comfortable for people. As he was going along to the south he saw some one coming toward him carrying a heavy load. This person had no eyes.

When the god saw him he said: "Eh, old man, the load has nearly worn you out."

The old man sat down, falling over as he did so.

"Help me carry it," he said.

"All right," said the god. "Push the load up on my back while I sit under it."

When the blind man pushed the load on the god's back he untied the strap by which it was held, so that the load fell. If the god had not jumped out quickly the load would have fallen upon him and cut him to pieces, for it was a load of sharp, black rock called obsidian, of which arrowpoints are made. The blind man felt around to see if he had killed the god, for this old man was in the habit of killing people by letting the load fall upon them, when they offered to help him carry it.

He could not find the body of the god, and he said to himself: "This one I did not kill."

Then the old man arranged the pieces of sharp stone in the bundle again.

Now the god spoke to him: "Come, it is your turn. Let me push the load on your back."

The old man was afraid, now.

"No, I will let nobody push the load on to me."

Nevertheless the god threw him on the ground and pushed the load of sharp stones on to him, so that they stuck into him and cut him all to pieces. In that way the god got rid of this bad cannibal who killed and ate people.

Further on to the south the god found a man who was trying to catch passing travelers with a hook. As the god came along he grabbed the man's hook and allowed himself to be drawn quite close to the bad man. Then he suddenly let go.

Then he said to the man with the hook: "Come, let me catch you with the hook."

The old man said, "No."

But the god took the hook out of his hand and caught him with it and killed him.

Then the god said: "People will travel the trails in safety now, since I have killed the cannibals."

Further on he saw some one making a seesaw. This man asked the god to sit on the seesaw. After the god did so he suddenly let it down with a bang. But the god was too quick for him and jumped off in time to avoid being hurt.

Then the god said to this bad man: "Let me seesaw with you."

The man objected, but nevertheless the god put him on the seesaw, which was of sharp stone. He let the seesaw down hard and this evil man was killed by it.

Another man who was splitting a log of wood tried to get the god to stand in the cleft, intending to let the log spring shut on him suddenly. This man, who was also blind, was a cannibal, too, and caught people this way. When he thought that he had caught the god he brought a big basket pot and set it where he thought the god's blood would be dripping after he had been squeezed in the log. Then he set the wedge in the log. He felt around for the body of the god but could not find it.

Then the god said to him: "Come, you step into the crack."

The blind man did not want to do this, but the god pushed him in, and let the log spring shut on him.

The god said: "When people are going to build a house they may split logs this way, but they must not kill people to eat, as this wicked person has been doing."

This god tried to arrange for indians to live forever, or at least to live again once after they had died. But people did not like this scheme and the god failed to arrange it, so that now people die and do not come to life again.

Finally, after he had done all that he could to make this world a comfortable place for indians to live in, he went away across the ocean and was never seen again. He lives there today.

The Origin of Death

The Origin of Death

Hawk Chief lived with his grandfather, Coyote. He used to hunt ducks far along the shores of Clear lake. When evening came he would lie down to sleep, and the next morning he would return to Coyote, bringing the ducks he had shot.

One night as he lay sleeping two Flint girls discovered him. The two girls were out seeking young men to take back to their village to feed to their people. But Hawk Chief looked so nice as he lay sleeping that they were ashamed to hurt him. Instead they lay down on either side of him, and played with him, and teased him, being careful not to wake him. Shortly before dawn they left.

When Hawk Chief woke up, he noticed their tracks and wondered who had visited him while he was sleeping. He went home with his ducks, but he said nothing to his grandfather. The same thing happened to Hawk Chief three other times, but always when he awoke there was no one near. A fourth time the Flint girls came, but this time they tarried too long, and at dawn Hawk Chief awoke and caught them. He fell in love with them at once. He asked them where they lived and they told him far away in the east.

"I will go and live with you," he told them. Then he gave them his ducks and they went away.

Hawk Chief returned home to his grandfather, but he did not bring any ducks with him. He moped around the house for four days, saying nothing. Coyote knew very well what was the matter, and, when on the fourth day Hawk Chief left, he knew where he was going. Hawk Chief traveled east until he got to the village of the Flint people. He found his Flint girls and married both of them. But Moon-Old-Man, who was the brother of the Flint girls and a very mean man, was angry at this marriage. He kept asking Hawk Chief to come and visit him.

"Come and enjoy a sweat bath in my house," he would say.

But the Flint girls advised their man not to go.

"He is laying a trap for you," they told Hawk Chief. "You had better not go."

But Hawk Chief decided that he would go.

"Why do you want to go and see that old man?" the girls asked. "He is mean."

When Hawk Chief arrived at Moon's house Moon treated him very nicely. After a while he asked Hawk Chief to go and hunt deer for him. Hawk Chief went and brought him back a deer, but the old man complained.

"I could hunt deer myself, if only I had a bow."

Hawk Chief went out again and came back with a bow.

Again Moon complained.

"That's no good. I can't do anything with a bow without arrows."

So Hawk Chief went out and brought him back some arrows. Still Moon complained.

"I don't want this venison. I'm tired of venison. I want to eat acorn mush."

Hawk Chief thought the old man was getting childish and whimsical, but he said he would go and bring him some acorns.

"You don't have to go far," Moon-Old-Man said. "There is an oak tree growing right on top of this house."

Hawk Chief did not know that Moon had made the tree grow there on purpose, and so he went out and climbed it. While he was shaking down the acorns Moon shot him through the smokehole and killed him. As soon as Hawk Chief died, Coyote knew of it. He went to the village of the Flint people and got Hawk Chief's body and carried it home with him. There he worked on him for four days with magic, until Hawk Chief came back to life.

Coyote then said to all the people: "That is the way it is going to be in the future when people die. They will come back to life in four days."

Meadowlark Man, however, didn't like this.

"No, it is not good that way," he said. "That man you brought back to life smells. When people die they ought to stay dead."

Coyote and Meadowlark Man argued for a long time, until, finally, Coyote, tired of arguing, said: "All right! Let's have it your way."

But some time later, when the people were having races and Meadowlark's boys were in them, Coyote put a rattlesnake on the trail. As Meadowlark's boys came running along the trail they were bitten by the rattlesnake, and they died. Then Meadowlark came to Coyote.

"You know, I think that's a good way, the way you said it ought to be, and people should come back to life after four days," he said.

But Coyote said: "No, no. Now it's too late. You wanted them to stay dead when they die. We fixed it that way. That's what we agreed. That's what we agreed. That's the way it's going to be."

Meanwhile Hawk Chief was ashamed because he smelled so badly.

"People say I smell," he complained. "I am ashamed. I don't want to live any more."

So he went to his house and lay down and died again. Then they burned down his house over him. All the people who were brave jumped into the fire and were burned to death. All the people who were cowardly did not jump into the fire. They stayed behind and they became the animals of today. The people who jumped into the fire woke up the next day in the land of the dead. Their house was right there in this land.

Then Coyote said to all the people: "When people die they are to come to my house in the land of the dead, beyond the ocean. They are to come there after four days. Only dead people are to come there, not live people. That's the way it's going to be."

That's the way it is. When people die they go to Grandfather Coyote's house in the land of the dead. That's way down south.

COYOTE'S DEATH

[As told by the Shasta indians of Siskiyou county]

Eagle sent down on this earth his two children, a boy and a girl, so that they would create people. They created children, and there came to be many people. No one ever died, and as more people were being created all the time, the world was becoming quite overcrowded. Everyone wondered what to do about it.

Then one day a boy died! The people gathered together and said: "Let us not die."

But Coyote said: "No! It shall not be so. People shall be sad; if a man's wife dies, he shall be sad and cry, but people must die."

They buried the boy therefore, but were angry in their hearts towards Coyote, wishing all the while that his child might die.

Coyote's child did die, but Coyote didn't want him to remain dead. He wanted to get him back. So Coyote followed his child to where the dead were. He found the ghosts of the dead dancing about a fire. Coyote then built a fire of wild parsnips, and as soon as the dead smelled it they gave him back his son.

When Coyote returned with his son to his house the boy said: "For ten years you must not beat me, must not scold me."

But after five years someone scolded Coyote's son and he died again. Coyote went again to the place of the dead. The dead were dancing, and when they saw Coyote they said to him: "Go back to your home, and day after tomorrow come back again for your son."

So Coyote went home alone this time, and went to sleep. The next day the people found that Coyote had died. Coyote had returned as the ghosts had instructed him, but only as a ghost not as a person.

So the example was set for all time. No one could follow the dead to their country, unless he went as a ghost himself.

MEADOWLARK STARTS DEATH

[Told by the Chukchansi indians of Madera county]

One day a person died. No one had ever died before, and the people did not know what to do. After some time the dead body began to give forth a bad odor. Meadowlark smelled it and he did not like it. So Coyote said: "I think I will make him get up." But Meadowlark said: "No, do not. There will be too many. They will become so hungry that they will eat each other."

Coyote answered: "That is nothing. I do not like people to die." But Meadowlark told him: "No, it is not well to have too many. There will be others instead of those that die. A man will have many children. The old people will die, but the young will live."

Coyote said nothing more, and so from that time on people have always died. But Coyote said to burn the body of the dead person, and it was done.

How People Got Fire

How People Got Fire

THE BURNING OF THE WORLD

[As told by the central Yana indians of Shasta county]

The world was full of busy people, hunting and killing deer, catching salmon, and gathering sunflower seeds. When the villagers returned from their day's work they would cook these foods. But it seemed as though the fire never thoroughly cooked the food; it would only brown it on the outside but the inside was still raw. No matter how long they cooked their food it never seemed to get done, and they had to eat it half raw.

"We do not like this fire," said the men in the village. "We are tired of eating raw deer meat. There must be better fire somewhere around here."

So the people came together to talk this matter over. They decided to have one man sit on top of the mountain every night and look all over the world for fire.

He looked to the east, to the north, to the west, but could see no fire. When he looked to the south, there he saw sparks rising. Down in the south was the fire they wanted.

He reported this to the assembled people.

"Let us go and steal it," they said.

Two men set out, traveling under the ground all the way. When they arrived in the south they came up out of the ground and set off for the fire village.

Coyote had been sleeping as they passed through on

their way to the fire village, but he woke up in time to see their departing forms.

"Where are they going to?" he asked first the rocks, then his cooking basket.

But they could not tell him.

Then he spoke to the acorn mortar: "Mortar Woman, where have the two men gone?"

"They are on their way to the fire village. They are going to get some fire and bring it back to the people in the north," she said.

Coyote wanted to be able to say that he too had helped bring fire to the people in the north, so he set out and followed in their tracks.

He soon overtook them. "Why didn't you tell me about it?" he asked.

They would not answer him, for they were angry at his following them. They wanted to be the only ones to get the fire.

They reached the fire village in the middle of the night. While all the people slept, the two men stole a chunk of burning coal. They started back to the north. Part of the way one would carry it, and part of the way the other.

As they made their way back to their own village Coyote followed, running after them and begging to be allowed a chance to carry the fire also.

"You might drop it down on the ground. You might burn your hand," said Fox, one of the men.

But Coyote begged for a chance to carry the fire, so that he might tell all the people that he had helped gain the fire. So Coyote was given the fire.

But the fire burned Coyote's hand and he quickly dropped it. It started to burn where he dropped it —

it spread farther and farther to the north, burning all the people and villages.

Meanwhile the two men who had first obtained the fire arrived back in their village, breathless and frightened.

"We've got to move," they cried. "Everything is burning up – the people are burning. But we can't move down into the ground, for the fire is burning the earth."

Eagle, the chief of the village, flew to Spider.

"Have you a strong rope?" he asked.

"Yes," said Spider. "Let all the people get into my big basket and I'll pull them up to the sky." Spider then said, "Stretch out," and the basket grew ever so big.

They all climbed inside of Spider's large basket and Spider tied the basket onto the sky and started pulling it up. Coyote stretched himself out on his stomach on the floor of the basket. Spider had almost reached the sky when Coyote remarked, "I am going to look down and see the fire, my friends."

"Look out," cautioned Eagle. "You might fall down."

But Coyote could not restrain his curiosity to see the fire.

"I shall just tear a little hole in the basket. I want to see how the fire is burning down there. I shall look down to the ground through a tiny little hole," he said.

So while Spider kept pulling at his rope, hoisting the basket nearer the sky and farther away from the burning earth, Coyote made a little rent in the tule basket.

He looked down and saw the fire.

Then the hole he had made began to grow larger.

The hole got bigger, until suddenly Coyote fell out! He went sailing down to the earth. Then all the people started falling out. They all fell down to the earth and burned up completely. Only Spider remained in the sky.

WHY THE INDIANS ARE ABLE TO GET FIRE BY DRILLING
[As told by the Karok indians of Humboldt county]

In the very beginning of things the Karok indians had no fire. Kareya, the creator, had made fire but he had hidden it in a box and given it to two old hags to guard. He did not want the Karok indians to get it. Coyote decided to help the indians by obtaining the fire for them. He called together all the people and told them what he was going to do. He then stationed them in a line along the road to the cabin of the hags who kept the fire. This done, he went with an indian to the cabin. As he neared the house he told the indian to hide under a hill near-by, while he went in.

He rapped on the door.

"Good evening," he said, as the hags opened the door to him.

"Good evening," they replied.

"It's a pretty cold night," he said. "Can you let me sit by your fire?"

"Yes, come in," they replied.

So he went in and stretched himself near the fire. He pretended to go to sleep, but all the while he kept the corner of one eye open, watching the hags. The hags did not go to sleep. They never slept for they guarded the fire night and day. As Coyote watched them he thought of how he would get the fire.

Next morning he left the cabin and went to the indian hiding under the hill.

"You must make an attack on the hags' cabin, as though you are going to steal fire, while I am in it," he told the indian.

Then he returned to the cabin. The hags had no fear that Coyote would try to steal the fire. They believed only the indians would try to get it. While Coyote stood close to the fire, the indian descended on the cabin. The hags saw him and dashed out of one door to attack him. Coyote at once seized a brand of fire and ran out the other door. He fairly flew over the road, the sparks from the fire flying about him.

The hags saw the sparks and gave chase. They had almost overtaken him when Coyote reached Mountain Lion, the first person stationed along the road. He gave him the brand of fire and Mountain Lion ran with it to the next person along the road. The hags continued to chase each one. The last one along the road was Frog, who could not run. So when Ground Squirrel, running with the fire, came to him he opened wide his mouth and swallowed the fire.

The hags were almost upon him, so he jumped into the water. They grabbed for him but only succeeded in catching hold of his tail, which they pulled off. That is why frogs today do not have tails.

Frog swam along under water, holding his breath so as to keep the fire. Finally, he could hold his breath no longer and had to come up. He spat out the fire into a log of driftwood, and then took a deep breath.

The fire has stayed in the wood ever since, and so now when an indian wants fire he simply rubs two pieces of wood together and the fire comes out.

DOG STEALS FIRE

[As told by the Achomawi indians of Shasta county]

After the flood people found that all fires were put out all over the world. Nothing could be cooked. After a while people began to be troubled about it, so they sent Owl to Mount Shasta to look all over the world and see if he could find any trace of fire.

Owl went, and reached the top at last, very tired, and wet with perspiration. He looked all about, and then he looked west twice. There he saw smoke coming from a house. He came back to the people and told them he had seen fire in the west.

Next morning all the people set out with cedar-bark torches, for the west, where the fire had been seen. Dog was along, and he carried some punk hidden in his ear. They arrived at the house where the fire was, late in the evening, and asked to be allowed to warm their hands. Dog held his ear down and the fire ignited the punk. Then, all the rest of the people thrust their torches into the fire, and ran out of the house.

The people of the house were very angry, and they caused rain to fall, so that it would extinguish the torches. Thus, when the people arrived home, their torches were all out. No one knew that Dog still had fire. They all sat around, looking very glum and troubled.

Dog began to laugh, and said, "I am sweating."

Coyote got angry at this. "Hit him! Knock him out!" he said.

Then Dog said to Fox, "Look in my ear."

When Fox did so, he saw the fire. He took out the punk and made fire from it. That is the way people got fire again.

MOUSE STEALS FIRE

[As told by the central Miwok indians of Tuolumne county]

A long time ago, in the very beginning of things, the people in the hills were freezing, for they had no fire with which to keep warm. They gathered in their assembly house to talk over what they could do. There were Black Goose, White Goose, Lizard, Coyote, Mouse, and many others. It was Lizard, sitting on the rock outside of the assembly house, who discovered fire emerging from an assembly house in the valley below.

Later, Mouse, the Flute-player, slipped away unnoticed to go and steal some of the fire from the valley people. He took with him four of his flutes. When he arrived at the assembly house in the valley he found Bear, Rattlesnake, Mountain Lion, and Eagle guarding all the entrances. But Mouse managed, nevertheless, to get into the house. He climbed on top of the house, and while Eagle slept he cut two of his wing feathers which were covering the smoke hole, and slipped in.

Once in, he began to play his flute for the people. The music soon lulled them to sleep, and, when they were all snoring, Mouse safely filled his four flutes with fire and escaped.

When the people awoke they searched all over the hills for the one who had stolen fire from them.

Eagle sent Wind, Rain, and Hail in pursuit, for they were considered the swiftest travelers among the valley people. Finally Hail came up to Mouse, but Mouse had concealed his flutes under a buckeye tree just before Hail overtook him, and so denied having the fire. Hail believed him and departed.

Because Mouse placed his flutes of fire under the buckeye tree, there remains to this day fire in the buckeye tree, and people today obtain their fire with a drill of buckeye wood.

After Hail's departure, Mouse resumed his journey with his four flutes of fire. He met Coyote, who had become impatient fearing some dreadful fate had befallen Flute-player, and had gone out to find him.

Arrived home, Mouse sat on top of the assembly house, playing his flutes and dropping coals through the smokehole.

Coyote interrupted him, however, before he was finished, and so it is that the people who sat in the middle of the house received fire. Those people now cook their food and talk correctly. The people who sat around the edge of the room did not get any fire and today when they talk their teeth chatter with the cold. That is the way the languages began. If Coyote had not interrupted and Mouse had been able to finish playing all his flutes of fire, everyone would have received a share of fire and all would have spoken one language.

Indians today talk many different languages for the reason that all did not receive an equal share of fire.

MOUSE REGAINS FIRE
[As told by the northeastern Maidu indians of Plumas county]

Thunder was always wanting to be more powerful than anyone else. One day he decided that if he could manage to get fire away from the people they would starve to death, because they would not be able to cook their food. Then he would have conquered the whole world.

After a time he succeeded, and carried the fire home with him, far to the south. Here he got Wowosim, a small bird, to guard it. He paid Wowosim beautiful beads for this work. And Wowosim wore the beads while he stood guard over the fire and sang, "I am the man who never sleeps." But the people did not die as Thunder had hoped. They managed to get along on raw food. Sometimes, however, the chiefs would get a certain small bird to look long and hard at a piece of meat; and as this bird had a red eye, it would, after a long time, cook the food almost as well as a fire.

One morning, Lizard, while sunning himself on the roof of the assembly house, looked off toward the Coast range mountains and saw smoke rising. He called to the people to come and see it.

"How shall we get that fire back? How shall we get it away from Thunder," they asked.

"He is a bad man. I don't know whether we had better try to get it or not," Lizard answered.

But the chief interrupted, saying, "Even if Thunder is a bad man, we must try to get the fire back. The best one among you had better try to get it."

Mouse, Deer, Dog, and Coyote were chosen to make the attempt, although all the people went along, too.

"I don't know how we shall get in when we get there, but the one who is best, who thinks he can get in, let him try," said Dog.

They took with them a flute in which to conceal the fire. They traveled a long time, and finally came within a short distance of the place where the fire was. Here they stopped to consider their plan of attack. They could see Wowosim, sitting on the top of Thunder's house. He was singing, "I am the man who never sleeps. I am the man who never sleeps."

Mouse was elected to see if he could get in. He crept

slowly up the side of the house until he was quite close to Wowosim. Wowosim had his eyes closed. He was fast asleep, even though he continued singing his song. So Mouse crawled to the opening and entered Thunder's house.

Now Thunder had several daughters. As Mouse entered he saw them all lying fast asleep.

Mouse thought, "Suppose they should wake up before I have a chance to escape?"

Then a scheme came to his mind. He stole up quietly and untied the waist-string of each girl's skirt, so that should they become alarmed and jump up, the skirts would fall off, and they would have to stop to fix them. Thus he would have a chance to escape. After this was done, Mouse took his flute, filled it with fire and then crept out and joined the people. The fire was given to the swiftest runner to carry. And so the people started back with their fire.

Meanwhile, Thunder awakened with a feeling that something was wrong.

"What is the matter with my fire?" he asked. Then he jumped up with a roar of thunder, as he realized that some of his fire had been stolen.

His daughters awakened at his roar, but when they jumped up their skirts fell off and they had to stop and fix them. At last they were ready and they set out with Thunder to give chase.

They took with them a heavy wind, much rain,and a hailstorm, so that they might put out any fire which the people had taken.

Thunder and his daughters hurried along. Thunder, however, soon outdistanced his daughters and caught up with the fugitives. But just as he was about to catch them Skunk shot at him and killed him.

He looked at the dead Thunder and said, "After this
you must never try to follow and kill people. You must
stay up in the sky and be thunder."
The daughters of Thunder saw what had befallen
their father and they did not follow any farther. So the
people went on safely, and got home with their fire,
and people have had it ever since.

HOW COYOTE STOLE THE FIRE
[As told by the Shasta indians of Siskiyou county]

A long time ago, when there was no fire, and all the
people were wanting it very badly, some one went to
Coyote and said, "Where Pain lives there is fire. Do
you hear? He and his people catch their game by starting fires which cause the animals to flee, in a bunch,
away from the fire and straight towards the path of
these people, who then kill as many as they want."
When Coyote heard this he told Chicken Hawk,
Eagle, Grouse, and Quail that he was going to get some
of the fire. He told each to stand at a different place
along the road to Pain's house. When he obtained the
fire he would run to where Chicken Hawk was and give
it to him. Chicken Hawk was then to run on to where
Eagle was. Eagle was to take it and run on Grouse's
place; and then Grouse was to run to where Quail was.
Quail was to run with it to safety and eventually bring
it to the people.
Coyote then wrapped himself in a blanket and set out
at once for Pain's house.
He found only Pain's children at home. The old
people were away, driving game with fire.
He went into the house.
"Oh, you poor children! Are you all alone here?" he
said.

"Yes, we are all alone," the children answered. "Our parents have gone hunting."

"I think you are Coyote," one of the children said. "Our parents told us that if anyone comes it will be Coyote."

Coyote answered, "I am not Coyote. Look! Way back there, far off in the mountains, is Coyote's country."

As he finished speaking he stretched his feet out toward the fireplace, with his long blanket in which he had wrapped himself when he set out.

"You smell like Coyote," said the children.

"No, I am not," he answered.

As he said this the blanket, wrapped around him, caught fire and began to burn.

Coyote jumped up and ran as fast as he could to where Chicken Hawk was. Pain's children ran after him. When they saw Coyote hand the fire over to Chicken Hawk, they continued after Chicken Hawk.

Chicken Hawk gave it to Eagle and Eagle gave it to Grouse, who in turn gave it to Quail. Pain's children were in hot pursuit, however, and they saw each time the fire changed hands.

When Quail got the fire he ran far away with it. He wanted to elude the Pains first, before returning to the waiting people with the fire.

But the Pains were following, crying, "Coyote has stolen fire."

Turtle was walking along the river bank when Quail saw him.

"I'll give you the fire," said Quail. "Here! Take it!" For just then the Pains came running up.

Turtle immediately put the fire under his armpit, and jumped into the water.

Pain shot at him, striking him in the rear.

"Oh, oh, oh! That is going to be a tail," said Turtle, as he dove deep down into the river.

The Pains waited for him to come up.

Coyote joined them.

"Where is the fire?"

"Turtle dove with it," they said.

"Curse it! Why did he dive with it?" Coyote said. He was very angry.

By and by when Turtle did not reappear the Pains gave it up and went away.

After a while, however, Turtle crawled out of the water on the other side.

Coyote saw him.

"Where is the fire?" he called out.

Turtle did not answer.

"I say to you, where did you put the fire?" said Coyote. "Curse it! Why did you jump into the water?"

"You keep quiet! I will throw the fire about," said Turtle.

So he proceeded to throw the fire about. When Coyote saw this he was glad. He told all the people, who came and got some. Coyote was the first to get fire and now we have fire.

The World Fire

The World Fire

WHY THE WORLD WAS SET AFIRE
[As told by the Lake Miwok indians of Lake county]

Snipe wanted to marry White Goose girl, but she wouldn't have him. Snipe became very angry at this. In fact, so humiliated and angry was he that he left home and went away towards the north, with a wicked purpose in his mind. As he traveled northward he held a stone in his hand. This he kept throwing away from him, and wherever the stone landed a fire started. Then the stone would come back to Snipe, and he would throw it in some other direction, and where it landed a fire started there, also.

Each time he threw the stone it returned to him, and, as he kept going along, everywhere behind him a fire was burning the whole world.

The mischief done, Snipe tried to save himself and escape from the burning world. So he flew up in the direction of the upper world. But just as he reached the gate the fire overtook him and he fell dead. A fitting end for a wicked fellow like Snipe.

THE WORLD AFIRE
[As told by the Lake Miwok indians of Lake county]

Weasel was very rich. He had a fortune in flat disks of clam shell, strung like beads, hidden in his house. Far and near he was known to be mean, and no one went near him.

Hawk Chief lived in a big house some distance away. Every day he hunted for ducks, which he brought home and shared with the others in his house. As he was leaving the house, one morning, to go on his usual hunt, his grandfather, Coyote, called to him.

"If you see Weasel's house, while you are hunting, don't go there! Be sure not to go there, for he is a very mean man."

But Hawk Chief did not heed his grandfather's advice, and when he came to Weasel's house, he entered, for he was hungry and wanted food. Weasel, however, was not at home. Hawk Chief looked around for food. He found squirrel meat and acorn bread hidden in the house, and also numerous strings of clam shell beads.

Hawk Chief first ate until he was satisfied, and then he stole away from Weasel's house taking with him all the strings of clam shell money, which he hid in the creek near his house.

When Weasel returned home that evening he immediately noticed the empty sacks, where he had kept his beads. For four days he cried, and then he went outside and built a fire. While he worked on the fire, he said aloud:

"Somebody must have wanted to see me, somebody who was not afraid of me, somebody with plenty of power."

When the fire was roaring away furiously Weasel stuck his spear in it. Then he pointed it in all directions, looking for the thief. Not being able to locate him, he became angry, and cried:

"Now, the world is going to be destroyed."

Then the whole world caught fire. The fire spread until soon it neared Hawk Chief's house. Hawk Chief became frightened when he saw the fire approaching. "What's the matter?" Coyote asked him.

"Give him back his beads! I don't want them! They are in the creek," said Hawk Chief.

So Coyote offered Weasel his beads.

"I don't want them! It's too late, now. You are all going to be burnt. It can't be helped now."

But while the world burned, Coyote was busy. He took an elk horn and bored a hole in it, after which he laid it away in a corner under some rafters. Then he got his little buckskin sack, where he kept the rain, and going outside struck it, with all his force, against a tree. Very soon fog appeared overhead, and turned to rain. For ten days and ten nights it poured, extinguishing the fire that was burning up the world. It rained so much that the water rose over the houses. Coyote had known that this would happen and that was why he had first bored a hole in the elk horn. When he saw the water beginning to rise he went inside the hole and there he stayed until the flood went down.

When Hawk Chief saw the water rising and slowly covering his house, he looked for Coyote to help him, and when he could not find him he called out.

"Grandfather, come and help me!"

But Coyote was singing inside the elk horn and did not hear him.

As the water, which had reached the smoke hole, came pouring in, Hawk Chief spread his wings and flew out of the house. He flew around the world four times, but he could see nothing but water everywhere. After the fourth time around he was very tired, and felt as though he would die if he couldn't find something to rest upon. At last he saw two Duck Old Men swimming about.

"Grandfathers, grandfathers, save me! I am going to die!"

"All right, boy, jump on our backs," they answered. The old ducks took Hawk Chief to their house and made him lie down. They fed him and nursed him and kept him there until he was well. By that time the flood had gone down. Hawk Chief gave each of the Duck Old Men a lot of bead money.

"Now I am going," he said.

"Thank you, boy. Thank you, boy," they said to him. "But why do you want to go back to that old rascal (referring to his grandfather, Coyote)?"

But Hawk Chief left the house of Duck Old Men and went around the world looking for his wife and his grandfather. He couldn't find anybody, for everything had been burnt and destroyed. Meanwhile Grandfather Coyote was wandering around also, looking for his grandson. He was feeling badly and lonesome.

"I ought to have helped him. Maybe he is dead now!" he kept saying to himself.

Hawk Chief came to a creek. He saw a man on the other side.

"Heh, who are you?" he called across.

"Who are you yourself," the man on the other side of the creek called back.

"But you, who are you?" Hawk Chief again asked. "You must be full of magic power to be going around like that when all the world has been destroyed."

"You must have some power yourself, to call at me like that," the other man answered. "What's your name, anyway?"

"My name is Hawk Chief."

"Grandchild, grandchild! You are my grandchild,"

cried Coyote, for it was he on the other side of the creek.

Coyote leaped across and took his grandchild in his arms and carried him home, and made him lie down and doctored him, and fed him, and took care of him for a long time.

Stories about the Sun and Moon

Stories about the Sun and Moon

THE STEALING OF THE SUN
[As told by the Kato indians of Mendocino county]

Four times Coyote went to sleep. The first time he slept with his head toward the west, the second time to the north, the third time to the south, and the fourth and last time with his head to the east. As he lay sleeping with his head to the east his forehead grew very warm.

"I dreamed about the sun," he said when he awoke.

Then Coyote decided to get the sun and bring it back for the people. He set off. On the way he met three mice, and he took them with him for dogs.

"My heart is glad because I found you, my three dogs," he told them.

When they arrived at the house where Coyote knew the sun was, he instructed his dogs.

"The sun is covered with a blanket and tied down in the middle of this house. I am going in and shall sleep there tonight. When all are asleep you must come in and chew off the straps that hold the sun. Leave, however, the straps with which I am to carry the sun. When you are through, poke me with your noses."

Coyote then went into the house.

"I do not want food, grandmother," he said to the old woman of the house. "I will sleep."

"Yes," said the old woman, and gave him a blanket.

Covering his head in it, Coyote began to sing: "You

sleep, you sleep, you sleep." Soon the woman fell asleep. After a while the mice came and poked Coyote.

"We have finished," one of them said.

So Coyote got up, took the sun, and carried it off.

Mole saw him do this and he called out: "He is carrying off the sun," but no one heard him for his mouth was too small. Then Lizard saw him. He took up a stick and beat on the house of the old woman, calling: "He is carrying off the sun."

The old woman heard this time, and she got up and started to chase Coyote.

As she neared him she called out to him: "Why did you take it? I was fixing it."

"You were hiding it," Coyote called back. "Turn into a stone where you are standing."

At these words of Coyote the woman turned into a stone. Then Coyote took the sun and cut it up, and from it he made the moon, the stars, and the sun. As he made them he told them when they were to appear.

To the morning star he said: "You shall come up just before day." To the sun he said: "You shall come up in the east in the morning, and go down at night. You shall be hot." To the moon he said: "You shall travel at night. You shall be cold."

The people were very grateful to Coyote for what he had done, and they brought him many presents upon his return.

SUN'S ARRIVAL IN THE SKY
[As told by the lake Miwok indians of Lake county]

Hawk Chief was going around complaining because there was no sun in the world. Sun had shut herself up

in her house, and no one could get to her, for the house
she lived in was built of stone and she would not come
out.

"I want the sun, grandfather. Why is there no sun?
I want the sun," Hawk Chief kept crying.

So Coyote went to see the two doves. He took his
walking stick and his little sack of beads, and started
trotting along the trail.

"My grandson wants the sun," he said to the doves,
when he arrived. "He doesn't like it all dark."

"All right, grandfather," the doves replied. "We
know where she lives. We have seen her house. We
know how to catch her for you."

The doves then got ready and set out for Sun's house,
Coyote accompanying them. When they spied Sun's
house in the distance, they stopped where they were
and waited, hoping that somebody would come out.
But nobody came out.

The two doves then decided to shoot at Sun's house
and thus make her rise up out of the smoke hole. Once
out of her stone house they could easily catch her. But
they started quarreling over who should do the shooting.

"You had better let me do the shooting," the older
dove said. "You might miss."

"You? You are too old. You can hardly see any
more," the younger one replied. "But my eye is good.
I am young. My arm is strong."

"All right, shoot then, and don't talk so much," the
older dove snapped at him.

The younger of the two doves took up his sling, put
a stone in it, and started singing as he whirled it. Then

he let fly. The stone sailed through the air towards Sun's house, striking it on one side, and breaking right through the stone.

Sun became frightened and started out of her smoke hole, rising in the air. She soon went back into her house when she saw that not much damage had been done; the stone had only broken the wall of one side of her house.

"There! Didn't I tell you. Didn't I tell you to let me shoot?" the older dove screamed. "Didn't I tell you you would miss? Now you watch me. Watch me, grandfather, and don't be afraid."

"Oh, I am not afraid," said Coyote.

Then the other dove took up his sling, and he sang the same kind of song while he was whirling it. Then he let fly! This time the stone hit the house of Sun right in the center. Sun rose through the smoke hole and went straight up into the sky, blazing light, and hung way up there in the middle of the sky.

Coyote got so scared when Sun went up that he jumped and fell over on his back, blinking and rolling his eyes with amazement.

"Well, well, well, well," he said. "Now my grandson will be happy."

WHAT SUN DID TO MEADOWLARK

[As told by the western Mono indians of Madera county]

Sun married Mourning Dove and they were very happy. Meadowlark, however, wanted to marry Sun. So one day Meadowlark came to Sun's house. She found sun's children, who were doves, in the house, but Sun and Mourning Dove were not there. They had gone out in search of food. Sun had gone hunting and

Mourning Dove had gone to gather black seeds. Meadowlark picked up the children and threw them out on the ground in the broiling sun. Doves now have red feet because of this exposure to the sun. Mourning Dove came home and found her children outside. She picked them up and brought them in. Upon entering her house she saw Meadowlark sitting there. She wondered why Meadowlark had intruded. Soon after Sun returned. When he saw Meadowlark he stood and looked at her, but refused to be enticed by her advances. Meadowlark became very furious at this. So she returned to her mother's house. She told her mother that Sun would have nothing to do with her. Then she set to work to bewitch Sun.

Sun became very sick because of the witchcraft that Meadowlark was practicing against him. He lay at home and became worse and worse. When he was nearing the point of death Humming-bird, the doctor, was sent for. He cured Sun.

As soon as Sun was entirely recovered he told his wife that he was going to Meadowlark's house and pretend to marry her, in order to obtain revenge for the sickness she had brought upon him. So he went to Meadowlark's place.

He built a house for Meadowlark and her mother. He made it very tight and covered it with pine needles glued together with pitch so that it would burn easily. When Meadowlark and her mother were sound asleep in the new house he set fire to it, and went out. Meadowlark jumped up and called upon the rain to fall, which put the fire out, but not until she was badly burned. Although Sun did not get his complete revenge, he returned home satisfied.

WHY MOLE'S HANDS ARE BENT BACK
[As told by the Achomawi indians of Shasta county]

One time Sun conceived the great idea of rolling along on the ground instead of in the sky. So she fell down from the sky just about sunrise.

But Mole saw what Sun was trying to do, and he ran and caught hold of her. He held her up as high as he could, while he shouted in a loud voice for the people to come and help him.

All the people came running when they heard Mole's excited voice. With much shoving and pushing they helped Mole shove Sun up into the sky again. Otherwise today we would not have Sun in the sky, but instead she would be rolling along on the ground.

It was from holding up Sun that Mole's hands are bent so far back.

A STORY OF THE SUN AND MOON
[As told by the northwestern and northeastern Maidu indians of Butte and Plumas counties]

A long time ago, in the days before indians lived on this earth, a brother and sister lived together far away to the east. They were Sun and Moon. Instead of rising every day and traveling over the world as the people wanted them to, they remained within their house, which was made of solid stone. Many people were sent to try and see if they could make the two rise, but all failed, for they could not even enter the house built of solid stone. At last Gopher and Angle Worm went.

When they arrived at Sun and Moon's stone house they stopped to consider how best to enter. Angle Worm made a hole in the ground, boring down outside and coming up inside the house. Gopher followed, carrying a bag of fleas. Once inside, Gopher opened his bag and let half of the fleas out. The fleas began to bite Sun and Moon, making them move around. Then Gopher let out the rest of the fleas. These made life so miserable for Sun and Moon that they decided to leave the house.

Sun said to her brother: "Both of us cannot travel together. Do you wish to travel by day or by night?" Moon replied, "You try traveling by night."

So Sun tried it; but the Stars all fell in love with her, and she could not travel because of their attractions. Sun then went back and told her brother that he must go by night. This he agreed to, and has done ever since. Sun traveled by herself in the day.

Far away to the north she built herself a big house of ice. The house was so large that it looked like a mountain, and no one could climb up and get in. Sun then started stealing people and bringing them to this house, and then killing them.

One day, while on her travels, she came upon Frog and her three children. While Frog was not looking she stole one of the children. Soon Frog missed her child. She hunted everywhere, but could not find her. Then two days after Sun came again to Frog's house and stole a second child. Now there was only one child left, and this Sun wanted also. But she knew that now Frog was probably watching more carefully over her last child. So this time she waited ten days before returning to Frog's house, hoping that by that time Frog would have relaxed her careful watch.

When she arrived at Frog's house, Frog was seated in front of the door making a basket.

"Why are you sitting here in this lonely place?" Sun asked.

Frog asked the same question, suspecting that this was the person who had been taking off her children.

"I'm traveling about because I am lonesome," Sun replied. "But I am harmless."

At this answer Frog said to herself, "That is always the way that you talk. You think that no one knows anything about you."

So they sat there, Sun and Frog, saying very little to each other.

Soon Sun said, "I am going now. I am going to see what sort of a country I can find near here."

Just as Sun started to go the last of Frog's three children came outside to play. Sun seized the child and ran off to her ice house in the north.

Behind her, as she traveled, she caused a patch of willow to grow, so when Frog, who had seen Sun steal her child and was frantically following, came to the willow patch she stopped to pick some and forgot all about what she had set out for. By and by she remembered, however, and ran on. But Sun succeeded in getting into her house just as Frog came up.

Frog tried to climb up the side of the ice house, but could not do it. She slipped and fell back after getting only halfway up. But she would not give up, and tried again and again. After many trials she succeeded in reaching the top.

She called to Sun. "This is what you planned to do, is it?"

Sun did not answer.

"Do you think that you are going to kill me as well as my children?"

Still Sun made no reply.

Frog continued: "Come up here and let me see if you are the sort that cannot be killed."

Sun then replied, "What can you do to me?"

Frog opened her mouth wide, as she answered, "Come up, and you will see what I can do." So Sun started up, but as she came up out of the entrance, Frog swallowed her quick as a flash. Then Frog crawled away to one side and lay there a long time, thinking and wondering what Sun would do. Soon she began to feel Sun moving about inside of her. Then she began to swell and grow larger and larger.

"If Sun keeps on growing larger and larger, and in this way conquers me, there will be people in this world who will steal," Frog said to herself.

Before long Sun had grown so much that part protruded from Frog's mouth, and, continuing to grow, she finally burst Frog in two, and killed her.

Because Sun, who had stolen Frog's children, conquered Frog, today there are people in the world who steal.

THE MOON'S PHASES
[As told by the Karok indians of Humboldt county]

Moon was disliked by everybody. Because of this he didn't care whom he chose for wives, and so he married Rattlesnake, Grizzly Bear, and Frog.

Many people visited Moon and tried to get rid of him. Lizard came nearest success, for he managed to start eating Moon, but just as he was nearly finished, Frog, one of Moon's wives, came upon him and chased him away. Then with some of Moon's blood, which Frog took from the little that was left of him, she made Moon over, until he was large again.

Lizard is always returning and eating Moon, and each time Frog Woman chases him away just in time and makes Moon over again. That is why, today, we sometimes see all of Moon, and then he gets smaller and smaller until he disappears from sight.

COYOTE AND THE MOONS (MONTHS)
[As told by the Shasta indians of Siskiyou county]

In the long ago, there were ten Moons. Now this state of affairs was not at all satisfactory, so the people gathered together and talked it over.

"The winters are too long because we have too many Moons," they said. "Shall we kill the Moons?"

Coyote, who was present, jumped up.

"Yes," said he, "and I am the one who can kill them. I will do it."

"All right," the people said.

Then they instructed him where to go. Far to the east, they said, the Moons lived. They were guarded by Toruk, a great bird, whom they had captured a long time ago, and who could not escape because the Moons had taken out his leg bones.

"Every day," the people told Coyote, "the Moons go to gather roots and leave Toruk in the house to guard it. When he is hungry he cries, and one of the Moons returns and feeds him."

So Coyote set out for the home of the Moons, taking some food with him.

"I will fool them well," he said to himself.

When he arrived at the Moons' house he found that they were away, gathering roots.

When Toruk espied him, he became frightened, and was about to call out in warning, when Coyote said: "Be still, it is a friend."

Then he produced the food which he was carrying.

"Here is food for you," he said. "Eat it, while I fix your legs."

So while Toruk ate the food, Coyote cut up some black oak trees and made him legs from the limbs. Then Coyote instructed Toruk.

"Cry out for food, for I want a Moon to come."

So Toruk cried: "To-o-o-o."

The Moons far away heard him.

"Ha, he is hungry," they said.

The Moon who was Rain was told to return to Toruk and feed him.

Toruk and Coyote knew he was coming for it began storming. Coyote hid behind the door and when Moon poked his head in the door he seized him by the hair and cut off his head.

Then he threw the head behind the door and the body to the other side of the house.

"Now cry again," he said to Toruk, while he warmed himself by the fire.

"To-o-o-o," Toruk cried.

The Moons far away heard, and said: "Oh, the slave is not satisfied."

A second Moon was told to return and feed their captive. This Moon was Hail. Coyote killed him in the same way he had the Moon who was Rain.

Again Coyote had Toruk cry for food, and this time the Moon who was the Strong Winds returned and was killed.

The next Moon who returned and was killed was Sleet. And still again Toruk was told to cry for food.

The Moons, hearing him again, said: "What is the matter with that slave? He is calling again."

This time the biggest Moon, who was Frost, was

told to go. When he approached the house it was so cold that Coyote was frozen stiff. Everything was frozen. However, Coyote managed to kill this Moon in the same way he had killed the other four.

But when Coyote threw his head away from him it passed too near the fire and its hair caught alight. Toruk immediately said: "They have smelled the hair burning out there where they are digging. Let us run away."

So Coyote and Toruk ran, and escaped.

If Coyote had not succeeded in killing these five big Moons we would still have the long winters these people had, for there would be five big Moons as well as five small Moons.

Coyote Stories

Coyote Stories

COYOTE AND RABBIT

[As told by the western Mono indians of Madera county]

Jackrabbit had a very pretty younger sister named Cotton-tail Rabbit. Coyote wanted to marry Cotton-tail Rabbit, but he was refused. He became very angry at this and threatened to kill and eat all the rabbits and make blankets of their skins. But the rabbits were not afraid. They told Coyote to keep quiet. Coyote said nothing, but a plan formed in his mind, whereby he would get rid of all the rabbits.

He suggested to the rabbits that he and they swing up and down on a sapling. The rabbits agreed. They started looking around for a suitable tree – a tree which would bend over enough for their swinging. That night Jackrabbit went out secretly and walked all over the world. On his way he encountered Prairie Falcon.

Prairie Falcon asked, "What are you seeking?"

"I am looking for a slim tree that can be bent over, so that we may play at swinging on it with Coyote," answered Jackrabbit.

Then Prairie Falcon said, "Coyote is trying to kill you, because you will not let him marry your sister. I will arrange a suitable tree for you right near the house."

So Prairie Falcon accompanied Jackrabbit home, and fixed a nice sapling for the pastime.

"Come out in the morning and swing on the tree. I shall watch you," he said as he left.

Early the next morning Jackrabbit went out and played on the sapling, swinging himself up and down. Then he called to Coyote, telling him that he had found a satisfactory tree. Coyote came out at once. He swung Jackrabbit up and down. He intended to let go suddenly, so that Jackrabbit would fly up into the air and come falling down so hard that he would be killed. But before he had a chance to let go Prairie Falcon appeared. He told Jackrabbit to get off and let him ride.

Coyote swung Prairie Falcon up and down. Suddenly he let go of the sapling and Prairie Falcon shot swiftly upwards and then fell to the ground so hard that he was instantly killed. But he did not stay dead. He revived himself and came to life again. Then he invited Coyote to mount the sapling.

"It is great fun," he said. "You see all kinds of stars and all kinds of animals."

Coyote mounted and Prairie Falcon bent the pole way to the ground. Then he quickly let go. Coyote sailed up into the air and came down, striking the ground with a thud, and died. Thus the rabbits were well rid of Coyote.

COYOTE AND OWL
[As told by the Hupa indians of Humboldt county]

A long time ago Owl used to get his deer meat by driving the deer into the river while he sat between their horns. But there was a time, when, after Owl had dressed the meat and packed it ready to carry home, Two-Neck, a terrible monster, would come along and carry it off for himself.

One day Coyote came to visit Owl, and perceiving no deer meat, asked, "Why have you no venison?"

"Something always takes it away from me," said Owl.

"The next time he tries that I will kill him," said Coyote.

So the next morning when Owl landed with his deer, Coyote was sitting in the brush ready to fight. As soon as Owl had his load ready to take home, Two-Neck came along as usual. But when Coyote saw what a horrible-looking thing Two-Neck was he decided not to come out. Two-Neck carried Owl's deer meat away with him.

Owl went over to the place where Coyote had been hiding, but Coyote was not there. When he got back to his house, however, he found him sitting with his legs stretched each side of the fire.

"I told you he was a terrible fellow," said Owl.

"Well, I will kill him tomorrow," said Coyote.

So the following morning Owl brought another deer to land. When the load was ready, Two-Neck came along. Coyote was watching ready to fight.

"Come lift the load on my back," said Two-Neck.

As Owl was lifting it up he jerked it back. Coyote jumped out then and struck the monster on the neck. The two heads fell off but jumped back again. Coyote slashed him all over with his knife, but could not kill him. Then he ran to the river and got a sedge and whipped him with that. Two-Neck, cut everywhere, died.

Owl and Coyote carried the meat home. When they had eaten, Coyote said, "Well, I am going to walk down the river a way."

"Very well," said Owl.

As Coyote was walking along he saw a woman coming toward him. When he met her he saw she was dressed all in white, and then on looking closer he was surprised to see that her dress was of deer fat. He killed her on the spot, for the sake of her dress which he ate. Coyote walked on till he came to a house, which he entered. Several boys were sitting there.

"Where are the old man and old woman?" asked Coyote.

"This morning the old man went up the valley and has not come back yet. After awhile the old woman went after him. Didn't you meet her?" they said.

"No," replied Coyote, but they came up to him and smelled him. "You have her odor about you," they said.

Then they attacked him and there was a fight. Over and over again he pushed them into the fire only to see them jump out again. When he was nearly dead with the exertion, they said, "You can't kill us, for our hearts hang in a row there in the smoke-hole."

Then Coyote jumped up, got their hearts, and threw them in the fire. The boys fell back dead.

A great quantity of venison was stored in the house and Coyote stayed until he had eaten it all. Then he went back to see Owl for whom he had killed so many people. Owl would never be troubled any more by Two-Neck or any of Two-Neck's people when getting deer meat.

When he got back to Owl's house he was surprised to see grass growing all over the roof, and over on the hillside he saw Owl climbing up a dead tree carrying something with him. When he got up with it, his wife began to boil it, for it was venison. Coyote did not realize it, but he had been away a whole year. The Owls now did not recognize him as their benefactor. When Owl saw Coyote approaching he held a piece of the venison in his fingers, and teasingly called, "Take it, Coyote, eat it." But he did not throw it down and Coyote could not climb the tree.

"Come down," said Coyote, but they would not. Then Coyote tried to shoot them, but he could not hit them. After that he tried to burn the tree by building a fire at its base, but the fire would not burn.

All the time the Owls kept saying, "Here, Coyote, take this, eat it," but they were only fooling him.

Finally Coyote said, "Owls you may become, since you have treated me so badly." Then they turned into real owls.

COYOTE'S SALMON
[As told by the Shasta indians of Siskiyou county]

In the village where Coyote lived they did not have salmon; but in the neighboring village there was much salmon. The people had built a fish weir and were drying many salmon.

One day Coyote said, "I had better go to the next village and get some salmon."

When he arrived at the fish weir the people there gave him a great pile of salmon. He lifted the load with difficulty on to his back and set off. But the load was heavy and the way was long.

"I guess I will rest," he said. "There is all day in which to travel. I will take a nap."

So he stretched himself out on the ground, placed the pack of salmon under his head for a pillow, and went to sleep. And while he slept the Yellow Jackets came near him.

"May he sleep soundly," they said.

Then they took away his pack of salmon and put in its place a bundle of pine bark, tied up.

About midday, Coyote awoke. He did not look at his pack, but picked it up and took a bite of it, thinking it to be the salmon. Instead his face came against the bark. He jumped up.

"Who is it that has done this?" he said.

He looked for tracks but could not find any.

"I'll fix that man, whoever he may be," said Coyote. Then he ran back to the people at the fish weir.

"Coyote is running hither," they said. "What can be the trouble with him?"

When Coyote came up he told them, "I was tired and went to sleep. When I woke up I discovered that my salmon had been taken. Some one took every bit of it away."

The people told him to remain for the night, and in the morning they gave him another big pack of salmon and watched him depart, loaded down with his burden. When he came to the same place he had stopped to rest the day before, he lay down in the same way, with his pack for a pillow.

"I wonder what will happen," he said. "I wonder who will come."

Then he pretended to sleep. Soon the Yellow Jackets came and lighted on the pack of salmon. Coyote saw them, but he didn't believe that they were the ones who had taken all his salmon from him.

"They always light on salmon that way," he said.

But as he watched he saw them finally lift the pack and then start to fly away with it. He jumped up and followed them; but he soon grew tired and had to give up. He then returned to the people at the fish weir.

"Oh, here comes Coyote again," they said as they saw him running toward them.

"It was an evil being who took it from me," he told them.

All the people gathered together and heard about it. They told Coyote to take another load of fish again and go to the same place and rest just as he had the other two times. Then they all hid in various places near Coyote's resting place and waited to see what would happen. While they were thus waiting, Turtle came along. Coyote laughed.

"Whoever told you to come?" he asked.

Turtle said nothing, but sat apart by himself.

"Why did you come?" said Coyote. "You ought not to have come."

But Turtle sat there, and paid no attention to Coyote, who laughed at him. After a while the Yellow Jackets came. They lifted the load as before and started to fly away, the people following immediately after them. The Yellow Jackets flew straight towards Mount Shasta. The people who followed soon began to get tired, and one by one they dropped out of the chase. Turtle, of whom Coyote had made fun, was the only one who did not drop out. He kept on going, passing on the way all those who had given up.

"I am not really running," he said as he passed.

The Yellow Jackets soon got to the top of Mount Shasta, with the load of salmon. They went into the mountain through a hole at the top. Turtle saw where they went, and he climbed up the mountain to the hole at the top. Here he waited until all the tired people came up. He showed them where the Yellow Jackets had gone. The people started a fire and fanned the smoke into the hole through which the Yellow Jackets had entered. They tried to smoke the Yellow Jackets out, but they did not succeed. All over the valley, at the foot of the mountain, the smoke was pushing its way out of many holes.

Coyote ran from one hole to the other, trying to stop the smoke from escaping, and so that it would suffocate the people inside the mountain. But as fast as he stopped one hole the smoke came up out of the valley floor in another spot. This was the beginning of the volcanic eruptions in Shasta valley.

They could not smoke the Yellow Jackets out, and so they gave it up.

HOW COYOTE GOT HIS CUNNING
[As told by the Karok indians of Humboldt county]

Kareya was the god who in the very beginning created the world. First he made the fishes in the ocean, then he made the animals on the land, and last of all he made a man. He had, however, given all the animals the same amount of rank and power.

So he went to the man he had made and said, "Make as many bows and arrows as there are animals. I am going to call all the animals together, and you are to give the longest bow and arrow to the one that should have the most power, and the shortest to the one that should have the least.

So the man set to work to make the bows and arrows, and at the end of nine days he had made bows enough for all the animals created by Kareya. Then Kareya called all the animals together in a certain place and told them that the man would come to them on the morrow with the bows, and the one to whom he gave the longest would have the most power.

Each animal wanted to be the one to get the longest bow. Coyote schemed how he might outwit all the others. He determined to stay awake all night, while the others slept, and so go forth first in the morning to meet the man, and get the longest bow for himself. So when the animals went to sleep, Coyote lay down and pretended to sleep. But about midnight Coyote began to get sleepy. He got up and walked around, scratching his eyes to keep them open. As the time passed he grew more sleepy. He resorted to skipping and jumping to keep awake, but the noise awakened some of the other animals, so he had to stop.

About the time the morning star came up Coyote was so sleepy that he couldn't keep his eyes open any longer. So he took two little sticks and sharpened them at the ends. With these he propped open his eyes. Then he felt it was safe for him to sleep, since his eyes were open and could watch the morning star rising. He would get up before the star had completely risen, for then all the other animals would be getting up. But in a few minutes Coyote was fast asleep. The sharp sticks pierced right through his eyelids and instead of keeping them open they pinned them tightly closed. When the rest of the animals got up Coyote lay fast asleep.

The animals went to meet the man. Cougar received the longest bow; Bear received the next, and so on until the next to the last bow was given to Frog.

The man, however, still had the shortest bow left.

"What animal have I missed?" he cried out.

The animals began to look about and they soon spied Coyote, lying fast asleep. They all laughed heartily and danced around him. Then they led him to the man, for Coyote's eyes were pinned together by the sticks and he could not see. The man pulled out the sticks from Coyote's eyes and then gave him the shortest bow. All the animals laughed. This made the man pity Coyote, who was to be weakest of all animals, so he prayed to Kareya about Coyote. Kareya answered, and gave to Coyote more cunning than to all the other animals. And so that is how Coyote got his great amount of cunning.

HOW COYOTE BROUGHT SALMON TO THE KLAMATH RIVER

[As told by the Karok indians of Humboldt county]

Although Kareya, in creating the world, had put many fishes into the ocean, none came up the Klamath river. The reason for this was that Kareya had built a great fish dam at the mouth of the Klamath river. He had closed it and given the keys to two old hags to keep, so that the salmon could not go up the river. The hags guarded the key night and day, and never slept for fear that someone might come and steal it.

The people did not know what to do to bring the salmon from the ocean up the river, and many were dying from lack of food. Coyote decided to help the people get the salmon up the river.

He went to an alder tree and broke off a piece of bark. Bark of an alder tree turns red and looks like salmon when broken off of the tree. So Coyote took this piece of red, salmon-looking bark and traveled down the river until he reached its mouth. Here he saw a cabin. It was the abode of the two hags.

He rapped at the door of the cabin, and when the hags opened it, he very politely said, "How do you do?"

The hags did not suspect that Coyote had come to steal the key, and so they invited him to sit by their fire. Coyote entered and seated himself in front of the fire to get warm. Very soon he took out his piece of alder tree bark and started nibbling on it. "See, he has some salmon!" said one of the hags. She arose and took down the key, which was hanging very high on the wall, and went out to get some salmon. Coyote saw her take the key, but this did not help him very much because it was too high for him to reach. When the hag returned with some salmon, she cooked it and then both of them ate it all without offering Coyote any.

Coyote stayed all night in the cabin. He pretended to sleep, but all the time he was thinking how he would get hold of the key. Morning came and he had thought of no plan.

One of the hags took down the key and started out again to get some salmon. Then quick as a flash a plan came to Coyote. He jumped up and darted under the hag, knocking her down, and causing her to fling the key a long way off. Coyote bounded over to it, seized it in his teeth, and ran out of the cabin. He raced quickly to the fish dam and opened it.

Thus all the salmon from the ocean were allowed to pass up the Klamath river, and the people had plenty of food after that.

COYOTE IS PUNISHED
[As told by the western Mono indians of Madera county]

Coyote was a very wicked man, and none knew this better than his own son, Grasshopper. Grasshopper knew that his father was scheming to marry his daughter, Grasshopper's sister. This was a very terrible thing and Grasshopper did not want to see his father do it. One day Coyote and his mother-in-law went to set traps for jackrabbits. They caught many jackrabbits in their traps, which they skinned, dried, and hung up. These skinned jackrabbits, however, all turned into men. On the way back Coyote went ahead of his mother-in-law and arrived home long before her. He told his wife that the skinned jackrabbits, who had turned into men, were planning to make war upon them and kill her mother. Then Coyote left, presumably to go back and meet the oncoming band of jackrabbits; but instead he returned to the place where he had left his mother-in-law and killed her himself.

After that he shot himself through the upper part of one leg, with an arrow, and lay down, pretending he was dying. This was done as a ruse to deceive the people into thinking that the jackrabbits had killed his mother-in-law and wounded him in a battle. When Coyote failed to return home, his wife sent Grasshopper, the son, to see what had become of his father.

Grasshopper returned and reported: "He has been shot in the leg."

All the while Grasshopper was wishing to himself that his father would die.

His mother seemed to know this, and she asked: "Why do you wish your father to die?"

Grasshopper replied, "Because he wishes to marry one of my sisters."

His mother was shocked at this news, but Grasshopper continued: "I am not going to allow him to do that."

Coyote's wife then went and fetched her husband. "I am going to die," he told her, as she brought him in. "When I am dead, wrap me in a blanket and place me close to the outside edge of the house in which you are going to cremate me -- not in the middle of it. Then set fire to the house, but as you depart do not look back, for you might see my ghost and die as a result."

His wife answered, "How are you going to be cremated, if I place your body on the outside of the house?"

Coyote readily replied, "When the house burns my blanket will catch fire."

This was all part of Coyote's scheme to marry his daughter. He would pretend to die, and then his wife would, as he had directed, place him outside of the cremation house, set fire to the house, and depart, not daring to look back for fear of seeing the ghost of her husband. He would then escape and return and marry his daughter.

But this was not to be. Grasshopper arranged the cremation house. Then when Coyote had died, or appeared to have died, he placed him in the middle of the house (inside), instead of putting him at the outside edge of the house, as Coyote had especially requested. Grasshopper and his mother then set fire to the cremation house and left. Coyote's wife would not look back, for she feared that Coyote's ghost would appear. But Grasshopper looked back. He saw Coyote running about in the burning house, which soon fell upon him and completely burned him up.

So it was that Grasshopper destroyed his wicked father.

COYOTE OUTWITS PORCUPINE

[As told by the northeastern Maidu indians of Plumas county]

One day, while Porcupine was lying hidden in a hollow tree, he saw coming towards him and running swiftly, Elk. Elk was running away from Fox, who had been out hunting and had given chase to him. As he passed by Porcupine's hiding place Porcupine shot at him and killed him. Porcupine then came out of his hiding place and stood around, thinking how he should skin Elk.

"I have no knife," he said. "I must hunt up a sharp stone and use that for a knife. I wonder why I shot him when I have no knife to skin him with and cut him up?"

Coyote, walking on a hillside near-by, heard Porcupine talking to himself. He wondered what it meant and ran down to see.

"What are you talking about all the time?" he asked Porcupine. "What are you saying to yourself?"

"I am talking because I have no knife," Porcupine answered. "I killed Elk and now I can't skin him."

"If you will give me half of Elk," said Coyote, "I will let you have my knife."

Porcupine said: "No, you ask too much. I'll give you one-quarter if you will let me have your knife."

Coyote agreed to this, and Porcupine took the knife and began to skin Elk, while Coyote sat on a rock and watched him.

When Porcupine had finished cutting the animal, and was about to pull off the skin, Coyote called out, "Stop! Let me tell you something good. Let us get out here and jump, and the one that jumps the farthest will get the whole Elk."

At these words Porcupine stopped. Then he said: "No, I won't do that. I can't jump."

Coyote replied: "Do you suppose a fellow like me can jump? But if you won't jump, let's wrestle."

Again Porcupine refused, and said: "No, do you think a fellow like me can wrestle? I cannot wrestle." Then Coyote said: "Let us run a race. You look as if you could run."

But Porcupine said: "No, I can't run."

Finally Coyote said: "Well, put the skin over Elk, and then we will run and see who can jump farthest over it."

Porcupine replied: "Do you think I can jump? But if you want to jump this way, I'll try. You begin. We must have two turns apiece."

Coyote went back a little way, trotted up to the skin, and hopped over easily. Porcupine came along, and barely succeeded in getting over. Coyote was glad and he clapped his hands and laughed. He thought he would surely win. He started on his second jump, but, just as he rose over Elk's body, Porcupine said to the skin: "Rise up!" and it rose, so that Coyote only barely got across. Then Porcupine jumped the second time and succeeded in jumping the farthest, and so won Elk.

He began to cut up Elk, while Coyote sat by and looked on. When Porcupine had the meat nearly all cut up he looked over and saw Coyote. Feeling sorry for him he cut off a piece of Elk's lights and gave it to Coyote. Then he went on cutting, with his back turned to Coyote. This wicked fellow then stole a quarter and a shoulder, and ran off, leaving his knife with Porcupine.

Porcupine piled up the rest of the meat in the hollow tree, and lived there for some time.

COYOTE'S SAD END

[As told by the Luiseño indians of Riverside and San Diego counties]

One day Coyote set out along the road with his bow and arrow. He came up to Frog, who was busily engaged in making a large granary basket. He circled to the back of her and stood there, an evil intention in his mind. Frog knew what he was thinking of doing. "My nephew, I believe you are thinking of killing me," she said.

"No, I am not," Coyote said.

Then Frog said, "If you shoot me with your arrow, wherever you hit me water will run out and drown you."

"No, I don't believe it," said Coyote.

So he made ready his bow and arrow and shot her. Then he ran away as fast as he could. As soon as the arrow struck Frog, the water began to run out. It rose higher and higher, all the time.

Coyote came to a tree and climbed into it. The water surrounded the tree and began to rise up and cover it. Coyote climbed higher into the tree, but he soon realized that death was near. He began to sing about his brother, his relatives, and friends. While he was thus singing, many birds came close about the tree. They told him that if he would jump down they would catch him on their backs and carry him safely to land. Coyote believed them. So he jumped down from the tree; but the birds did not catch him as they had promised, and he fell into the water and was drowned.

And so Coyote paid the price of death for his wickedness in killing Frog.

The Land of the Dead

The Land of the Dead

THE ISLAND OF THE DEAD
[As told by the Tachi indians of Kings county]

A long time ago a woman died. Her husband buried her, but he could not bear the thought of her death. He wanted to get her back. He knew that very soon she would leave the grave and go to the island of the Dead. So he dug a hole near her grave and stayed there, watching.

On the second night he saw his wife come up out of the ground, brush the earth from her, and start off to the island of the Dead. He tried to seize her but he could not hold her. She slid through his hands and went on. He followed and attempted many times to hold her, but she always escaped.

Once when he had overtaken her, only to have her slip through his fingers, she turned to him and said, "Why are you following me? I am nothing now. Do you think you can get my body back?"

"I think so," he answered.

"I think not," she replied. "I am going to a different kind of a place, now."

The woman then went on, saying nothing further to her husband who continued following her. Soon they arrived at a bridge. On the other side of the bridge was the island of the Dead. The dead had to pass over this bridge in order to arrive at the island. Sometimes when the island became overcrowded with dead people, the chief would send a little bird to the bridge. As the dead walked along the bridge, the bird would suddenly flutter up beside them, which would frighten them and cause many to fall off the bridge into the river. There they turned to fish.

The dead wife passed over the bridge and entered the island. The chief of the island approached her.

"You have a companion?" he asked.

"Yes, my husband," she replied.

"Is he coming here?" he asked.

"I do not know," she answered. "He is alive."

Then the chief sent his men to the husband on the other side of the bridge.

"Do you want to come to this country?" they asked.

"Yes," he said.

They replied, "Wait. We will see the chief."

So the men went back to their chief.

"He says that he wants to come to this country," they told the chief. "We think he does not tell the truth. He intends to get his wife back."

"Well, let him come across," the chief answered.

He intended to send the bird to the bridge to frighten the man as he crossed, and so cause him to fall into the river. But the bird was not able to scare the man, and so he soon arrived on the other side and entered the island of the Dead.

The chief did not want him to stay. He said, "This is a bad country. You should not have come. We have only your wife's soul, and we cannot give her back to you."

But the man stayed on the island for six days, and watched the dead people dancing all the time.

Then the chief sent him home, saying, "When you

arrive home, hide yourself. Then after six days, come out and make a dance."

So the man returned to his parents.

"Make me a small house. In six days I will come out and dance."

But the man was in such a hurry to come out and tell all the people of what he had seen in the island of the Dead that he came out on the fifth day. He danced all night, telling the people about the island. He told them that even though the little bird who was sent to the bridge did all he could to keep too many people from entering the island, every two days the island became full. Then the chief would gather the people and say to them: "You must swim." The people would stop dancing and bathe. While bathing the little bird would appear and frighten them, causing some to turn to fish and others to ducks. In this way the chief made room for the new dead who were continually coming over the bridge.

Early in the morning the man stopped dancing, and went to bathe. There a rattlesnake bit him and he died. So he went back to the island of the Dead and he is there now.

It is through him that we now know about the island where the dead go.

THE RETURN FROM THE LAND OF THE DEAD
[As told by the western Mono indians of Madera county]

There once lived a man who had a very beautiful wife, and she died. They buried her after much mourning and she went up to the world of the departed. The man sorrowed deeply over the loss of his young wife, and finally set out to recover her. But his quest led him through many dangers. First he encountered fleas, innumerable fleas, which nearly bit him to death. He managed to get past them, however, without being killed. Then he encountered ants of many kinds, but after much suffering passed through them, also. As soon as he got through one horrible thing, another thing confronted him. There were hornets, gnats, horse flies, gopher snakes, water snakes, rattlesnakes, foxes, raccoons, dogs, coyotes, wild cats, bears, and wolves, all blocking his path, endeavoring to kill him. Nevertheless, he passed through all of these.

When he came to Wolf's camp, Wolf told him to take some sand in his hand and wade through the river, dropping the sand as he went along, so that he would not sink in the deep water. Wolf also warned the man that, when he came to Coyote's habitation on the other side of the river, he was not to smoke Coyote's pipe when it was offered to him. Neither was he, when he arrived in the land of the dead, to participate in any dance there.

"Do not talk to your wife, when you arrive there," said Wolf. "Just walk by and touch her on the shoulder with your elbow, and she will know that you want her to follow. Then return the way you came. When your wife walks behind you she will talk to you and try to get you to look back; but do not do that under any consideration. When you arrive at home your wife will go to her grave. Send her mother out to get her, for you must not talk to her for ten days."

The man followed Wolf's instructions and returned with his wife. However, he failed to observe the ten days' taboo against conversation. Before the ten days were up he spoke to his wife. She immediately returned

to the other world, and this time he could not get her
back.

WHY WE ARE NOT ABLE TO VISIT THE DEAD
[As told by the Shasta indians of Siskiyou county]

Once upon a time Woodpecker fell into the fire and
was burned to death. Her husband saw what happened,
but he could do nothing to save her. As he looked at
the fire into which she had fallen and burned up, he
thought he saw her ghost rise up toward the sky. He
went out in back of the house until he found the trail
of the ghost. The trail led up and up, until it was lost
in the sky.

Woodpecker's husband followed the ghost of his wife
along this trail until he reached the sky. He saw the
ghost proceed along the milky way. He tried to overtake her to catch her and bring her back to earth with
him, but during the day she far outdistanced him. In
fact, she left him far behind in the trail. When night
came the ghost camped on the trail and then her husband would almost come up to her. But always, before
he could reach her, the day commenced and she set off
again.

Finally the ghost reached the Other World, and soon
after her husband came. He found all the dead people
dancing and having a fine time, his wife's ghost included. He watched all this for a long time, then he
addressed the firetender.

"May I get back my wife?" he asked.

"No," the firetender answered.

After awhile he fell asleep; and when he awoke it
was daytime and all the dead people had gone to sleep.
They looked like patches of soft white ashes on the

ground. The firetender then approached Woodpecker's husband and handed him a poker.

"Poke the various sleeping ghosts," he said. "The one that gets up and sneezes when you do this will be your wife."

So Woodpecker's husband followed this advice. He found his wife and picked her up and started home. At first she weighed nothing, but as they approached the earth she grew heavier. She grew so heavy that before he was able to reach his house he dropped her. The ghost immediately ran back to the Other World.

Woodpecker's husband then started all over again along the trail to the Other World, and, as the first time, succeeded in getting hold of his wife in the Other World. But again, as he neared home, he was forced to drop her, because of her heaviness, and again the ghost ran back to the Other World.

A third time Woodpecker's husband followed his wife to the Other World. This time, however, the firetender told him that he might not try again.

"Return home, and in a short time you will be allowed to come and live with your wife," he told him.

So Woodpecker's husband was forced to follow these instructions, and returned home and went to sleep. He died, and then as a ghost returned to the Other World for good.

If Woodpecker's husband had succeeded in bringing back safely to our world the ghost of his wife, today everyone would be able to visit the Other World without dying first.

Stories about Monsters

Stories about Monsters

PELICAN THE MURDERER
[As told by the Salinan indians of Monterey county]

Long, long ago, Raven and Prairie Falcon heard of a murderer, Pelican by name, who lived far away.

Pelican would stand by the door of his house and when a man came by he would invite him to pass the night in his house. Then when his guest went to sleep he would place his bed near-by. When he heard the guest snore he would go over to him and ask three times, "Are you asleep?"

If he got no reply he would drive his long bill into his guest's heart and thus kill him. That was the way Pelican killed all his victims.

Raven and Prairie Falcon decided to rid the world of this wicked man, and so one day set out for the place where they knew Pelican lived and carried on his wicked practice. Pelican greeted them and asked them what they wished.

"We wish shelter for the night," they replied.

"You may both sleep here," Pelican replied, and so they remained.

When they got into bed they slept only a little, and then they got up and put in their places two logs of wood. They hid themselves near, and pretended to snore.

When Pelican heard the snoring, he arose and said, "I will go and kill them!"

He came up close to the bed, and asked, "Are you asleep?"

He asked this three times, and, as he received no answer, he was certain the two guests were sound asleep. He then raised his bill, and with a mighty stroke, dug it into what he supposed to be his guests. But he hit, instead, the logs, and split his head all to pieces. He fell dead. Raven and Prairie Falcon then jumped up.

"That is the way he always did in order to kill people," they said.

Thus was the world rid of Pelican, the murderer.

THE TWO-HEADED MONSTER
[As told by the Chilula indians of Humboldt county]

In a far away village, where once many people had lived, there now reigned a two-headed monster. The hillside leading from the forest down to the creek was white with the bones of people killed by him.

In another village four brothers and an old woman lived. One day the oldest and wisest of the brothers decided to go down to the creek. He set out and finally came to the creek. While walking along its bank he heard something making a noise on the hill on the other side of the creek. As he kept on he wondered what it was that was making that noise.

Then the two-headed monster appeared from out of the hill-forest and proceeded to chase him about. He ran, but soon his breath gave out, and he felt as though he was about to die. Still the monster chased him and he was forced to continue running until he dropped dead from lack of breath. The monster then picked up his body and carried it across the creek and up the hill to the house where he lived. This house was so covered with moss that no one could see it. The beings who eat people lived there.

Meanwhile the old woman and the three remaining brothers became worried when the brother did not return. When two days passed and still he did not return, another of the brothers set out. Soon he came to the bank of the creek and headed to the north, as his brother had done. And then, like his brother, he heard something making a noise. It was the monster, who when going along made a noise in the forest like the blowing of the wind. The monster killed this second brother also, and carried him across the stream and up the hill to the house hidden by moss.

When neither the first nor the second brother returned, the third brother made ready to go. He never returned.

Now there was only the youngest brother left, with the old woman. He was only a little fellow, yet he said to his grandmother: "Today I am going."

She replied, "My grandchild, why do you say that? They will eat us all."

But he would not stay, and when the grandmother saw this she looked for his belt. When she found it she took it out and bade him put it on. It was very wide. "When you are about to lose your breath do this way," she told him, motioning for him to loosen his belt.

So he started out, following the same direction as was taken by his three brothers, who had gone off and never returned. When he came to the bank of the creek and was walking along he heard something making a noise. Off across the creek in the hill-forest the redwood trees were moving back and forth. It was the coming of the monster. When the monster saw him he started after him, chasing him around and around, until his breath was nearly gone. When he was almost about to die, he loosened his belt, as his grandmother had told him, and the monster fell apart, dead! It was the magic thing in his belt which had done it. Then the young brother went across the stream and followed the track up the hillside, covered with the bones of people killed by the monster, to the house hidden by moss. He went in.

An old woman and a boy were sitting there. Beside these two lay a net, made for catching the people which these persons ate.

"Something made a noise," the boy said to the old woman. Then he turned to pick up the net, but the younger brother loosened his belt, and the boy fell in two parts.

The old woman then took up the net, and the young brother did the same thing to her, and she died.

The young brother said, "People shall not live this way. They shall not eat people. They shall live right."

He set fire to the house and burned it. Then he set out to the southward, where his grandmother lived.

"I have come back, grandmother," he said.

"I am glad you came back, grandchild," she replied.

"I killed them," he said, and returned the belt to her.

"My body is glad," she said.

Her grandchild was left to her and they lived well after that.

TAKWISH, THE CANNIBAL SPIRIT OF MOUNT SAN JACINTO

[As told by the Cahuilla indians of Riverside county]

[As one travels eastward from Banning, in southern California, down into the Imperial valley, he passes right below a great mountain on the south side of the pass through which the rail and automobile roads run. This great mountain is San Jacinto. It towers more than 10,000 feet above sea level.

In a canyon on this great mountain is the home of Takwish, an evil spirit, who is believed to carry away the souls of people and also their bodies at times. Takwish is seen by people at different times. Sometimes he appears as a person. At other times he appears as a ball of fire, the electric meteor, which dashes along close to the ground. Takwish is always on the lookout for people, whom he can steal or whom he can rob of their souls. In his home on San Jacinto he feasts upon his human victims. His home is believed to be a large rock through which he can see as plainly as we see through glass. The tribes that live in sight of Mount San Jacinto all have stories about this evil being.]

Once upon a time a girl went to bathe in a pool near Takwish's house.

Takwish saw her and he stole her and took her to his house in the rock. He treated her as his wife, and for several years she lived there with him, feeding on human souls which Takwish brought back from his hunts. But she became very tired of eating souls. Then Takwish decided to let her return home. But he warned her, however, that for three years she must not tell anyone where she had been, or she should surely die.

He took her back to where he had first found her and from there she went home. Everyone was very happy to see her again. They asked her where she had been, but she remembered Takwish's warning and refused to tell. This made the people more curious and they kept asking her for a whole year.

Finally she told them all to gather together and then

she told them everything that had occurred to her while she was with Takwish. The next morning, just before sunrise, she died, as Takwish had said she would.

[Occasionally, a rumbling sound is heard issuing from the canyon where Takwish lives in his rock. Then it is said that some girl is begging Takwish to let her go and that he is growling at her.]

THE CANNIBAL HEAD
[As told by the northwestern Maidu indians of Butte county]

A man once had a horrible dream. He told his wife that he had dreamed he ate himself.

The next day he and his family went to pick pine-nuts. They came to a tree laden with many nuts. He climbed the tree and started picking them. After a while he came down and made his son go up. While the lad was picking the nuts he dropped one of the pine-burrs. It hit his father on the leg, causing a flesh-wound, which started bleeding.

First the man wiped the blood away. Then he began to lick it. It tasted good, and he at once began to tear off pieces of his flesh and eat them. He kept on tearing off his flesh and eating it until nothing was left of him but his head and shoulders.

Then he began to bounce and roll about, only head and shoulders now, killing and eating people. Everyone ran away from him. Finally, he bounced into the river, and since then has never been seen.

THE ROLLING SKULL
[As told by the central Yana indians of Shasta county]

Wildcat's wife had just given birth to a baby, so Wildcat did not go deer-hunting, as usual. Instead he went with his wife and child to gather pine nuts. They came to a place where there were many trees loaded with pine nuts.

"I shall climb up for them here," said Wildcat. He climbed the tree and began throwing the pine cones down one after another. While doing this he began thinking of a dream he had had the night before. He dreamt that he was throwing himself down from a tree. So now he threw down one shoulder, then the other. Then he threw down one thigh, then the other. Then he threw down his backbone, until he had nothing left but his skull. Meanwhile, below, Wildcat's wife noticed blood dripping from the pine tree. She looked up and became afraid and ran off home.

"I don't know what he is going to do," she cried. "He has thrown his own members down, and bounds about in the tree with nothing but his skull. Blood is dripping down from the tree. I am afraid."

All the people were afraid!

"Let us run off to save ourselves," they said. "He might cause us all to die." So they ran away to the south, and hid in a sweathouse. They put a sandstone rock on the roof to keep others out.

Meanwhile, Wildcat's skull was calling to his wife. Upon receiving no answer he bounded down to the ground. He saw his child, left by his wife when she had fled in terror, and swallowed it. Then he bounded home only to find there were no people there. He bounded about to every house, but there were no people anywhere. He was very strong and cut up brush and trees as he went along.

"Ah! Where is it that you have all gone, running away to save yourselves?" he cried. "I'll find you."

He bounded about until he found their tracks, and then followed them to the south. He bounded along until he arrived at the sweathouse.

"Let me in, you people, I want to enter," he called. The people inside whispered to one another, saying: "Don't say anything. Don't let him in."

Again the skull called: "Let me enter, you people."

Again the people said to each other: "Don't let him get in."

When he saw that the people would not let him in the skull went some distance away and then with a great rush came back intending to burst into the house. But he could not, for it was too strong. He tried this many times, but, although the sweathouse shook, it was too strong for him to break in.

Suddenly he got an idea. He bounded high into the air, intending to burst into the house through the smoke-hole. But he was not able to because of the sandstone rock, which the people had placed over the opening. Wildcat's skull then bounded down and lay on the ground.

"Why should I try to burst into the house?" he asked. "It is too strong for me. Whither now shall I go?"

He bounded north and met some people. He killed them and went rushing on. He met more people and killed them, rushing on as before.

Coyote, who was coming along, heard the rushing sound, and said: "That must be the human skull. I am going to meet him. I hear that he is killing the people."

As Coyote neared the skull he began to sob. The skull lay quiet a while, listening to the person crying. Coyote stopped in front of it and said: "I hear that you were bad in the south. Why are you acting that way?"

The skull spoke.

"I dreamt that I threw my body down. I dreamt that I was bounding about, merely a skull."

"I have seen a person that way before, acting like you because of a bad dream, and I have caused him to be a person again," said Coyote, speaking to the skull, who lay there, big-eyed, consisting of nothing but his eyes.

Then Coyote continued.

"I put wood and rocks into a hole, and I built a fire down in the hole. When the rocks were hot, I got some pitch and smeared that skull with it, and then I put it down in the hole. When the pitch had all sputtered away that skull stretched out until it became a person again."

Wildcat's skull begged Coyote to do the same thing to him. But when Coyote placed him in the fire hole and he became heated, he attempted to burst out, but could not, and so died.

THE ROLLING HEAD
[As told by the Shasta indians of Siskiyou county]

Once, long ago, some children, twelve of them, were digging camas bulbs and they found a human head. One of the girls snapped it with her digging stick, as if she were playing a game.

"Why do you do that?" exclaimed one of the girls, and she started crying. "It is like us."

This girl then, with the help of one of the boys, buried the head and covered it over with earth. After the children had finished digging camas they went home. As night came on they started a round dance. In the midst of this dance, the two children who had buried the head saw something that looked like fire rolling along towards them.

"An Evil Being is coming," they cried. "It is the head. Let us run away."

So all the children gathered up their belongings in a great hurry, and ran away. The head rolled after them. But it wished the children to go to sleep, so it stayed out of sight. About midnight the children, not seeing the head any more, felt they had escaped from it, and they decided to sleep. But the same two children, who had first given the warning, woke up and saw the head approaching.

"Get up!" they screamed to their playmates, and ran away. But the other children did not hear. They were sleeping too soundly. The head was now almost upon the sleeping children.

"Ts-ts-ts," it said, and ate the eyes of all the sleeping children.

Then it started after the two who had run away. But those two had reached Coyote's house.

"Old man," they called out to him, "there is an Evil Being coming."

Coyote let them in, and when they told him who the Evil Being was he quickly put stones in the fire, placed a pail of water near-by, and then made his bed. Then Coyote and the two children looked out of the window along the trail. Very soon they saw the head approaching. Coyote immediately went to the fire, took out all the stones, which he had put in, and placed them under the bed.

The head came to the door of Coyote's house.

"Halloo, my son-in-law," it said to him. "Where are my daughters?"

"They are there on the bed," said Coyote. The head came in and sat down on the bed. Coyote leaned over towards the pail of water and kicked it over. The head at once fell through the bed onto the hot rocks, and was thus killed. Coyote then said : "People shall not do like this when they are dead. When they are dead they shall be dead forever. Heads shall not follow people." That is all.

HOW WINGI WAS DESTROYED
[As told by the Serrano indians of San Bernardino county]

There once lived in a rock on the hill near the village of Wingi the spirit Tuit. All the people in the village were very much afraid of Tuit, and kept out of his sight. They would make their children stay indoors after dark, so that Tuit could not run off with any of them.

Now it happened that one little girl in the village, Pahalali by name, cried incessantly. Finally, her mother, in anger, threw her out of the house. Tuit, the spirit, immediately appeared and took the little girl to his house. Here Gopher lived with Tuit, and Pahalali grew up along with Gopher. She never saw Tuit, all the time she was there, but she did see fire and smoke quite frequently in the house. This was really the spirit. One day the girl asked Gopher about her mother.

"The spirit is not your mother," Gopher said.

"I should like to go to my mother," the girl said.

"You can go," Gopher replied, "but the spirit may kill you. I will make two holes for you to escape."

Pahalali wanted to go and so she followed Gopher's instructions and escaped. She went back to Wingi. The people there asked her whence she had come.

"My mother told me when I was small that a spirit would get me," she replied. "He did get me and raised me."

The people were all very glad to see her, and her mother took her into her house again.

After dark the spirit came home and called for Pahalali. When she did not come he asked Gopher about her.

"I saw her playing here but a short while ago," Gopher said.

The spirit then threw into the air a magic basket to determine in which direction the girl had gone. The basket started to travel, and the spirit followed, for he knew that the basket would lead him to the little girl.

Meanwhile, Gopher sent a message to Pahalali.

"Tell your mother to put you in a bundle and place you in the 'big house.' Have all the people watch you. The spirit is going to look for you and try to kill you."

So Pahalali's mother put her in a bundle and placed her in the "big house."

Then Gopher sent another message.

"Tell your mother to heat a stone very hot. When the spirit asks for you, she must tell him to open his mouth to receive you. Then she must shove the hot stone into his mouth."

So when the spirit, following the basket, finally arrived at the door of the "big house" he knew that here Pahalali was hidden. He asked for her.

The girl's mother answered him.

"Open your mouth for Pahalali," she said.

As he did so she threw the hot stone into it.

"Haa!" the spirit shouted in pain.

He kicked in the house and ate all the people, and then died with the hot stone in his mouth.

Thus did Tuit destroy the village and the people of Wingi.

CHIPMUNK, THE GIANT-KILLER

[As told by the central Miwok indians of Tuolumne county]

Yayali, the giant, set out in search of food. He searched everywhere, over all the hills, shouting in a deep, loud voice as he went along. He started up the mountain, looking all the time for someone to eat. Far up in the mountains Chipmunk, thinking that his wife's brother was approaching, answered the giant's call and went to meet him. When he approached and saw who it was coming toward him he knew indeed that he had made a sad mistake. The giant made Chipmunk lead the way to his house, although Chipmunk tried in vain to get the giant to enter the doorway before him. But Yayali would not hear of it.

"You are the owner of the house," he said. "You lead into your own house. I am not the owner of it."

As Chipmunk led the way to the door the giant reached into his basket for a stone, which he threw at Chipmunk, striking him on the back and killing him.

After he had killed Chipmunk, the giant called to Chipmunk's wife to help him bring in the meat. He then made himself at home and married Chipmunk's widow. Chipmunk's widow had a daughter whom she hid in a pit, fearful lest the giant discover the child and eat her.

Every day the giant left to go into the hills in search of more people. As he departed he rolled big boulders against the door, against both ends of the house, and also one over the smoke hole at the top of the house, where the smoke emerges. This was so his wife could not escape. Then he went into the hills to capture more victims.

When he returned he would say to his wife, "Cook and eat this food, or I will kill you." She answered always "Yes," and the giant thought that she ate the fat people, but instead she ate the deer meat which Chipmunk had provided for her.

After some time she gave birth to two giants. When the giant had departed for the day in search of food and while the two little giants slept, she would take her daughter from the pit and hold her in her lap. The thought of Chipmunk's sad end depressed her and used to make her cry all day, while the giant was away. When he returned in the evening, she hid her daughter in the pit again. She feared the giant, but she could not escape, because the boulders which the giant put against the doors were too heavy for her to push away. So each day she sat in the house and cried.

Far away in another place Chipmunk's brother dreamed about him one night.

"I think I will visit him," he said. "I will see how he fares. I dreamed that he was sick."

So he set out for his brother's house, telling no one that he was leaving. At last he arrived only to find the house blocked by the large boulders.

He called out to his sister-in-law, "I have come. Why are these large boulders against the door?"

Then his sister-in-law answered from within, saying: "Come in. The giant killed your brother. He closes the door with those large boulders each time he goes out."

He rolled aside the boulders at each end of the house and entered. His sister-in-law told him that the giant had killed his brother and she pointed out to him the giant's two sons. Her brother-in-law then inquired about her daughter, and she told him that she had placed her in the hole so that the giant would not discover and eat the child.

Then he told her to crush some obsidian. He said, "I am going to help you escape. But the giant has many brothers, who will probably follow you and try to catch you, while you are on your way home. Throw the crushed obsidian in their eyes. I shall not go with you. I shall remain here."

Chipmunk's brother next killed the two young giants, hitting them with a stick "in the ankle," the place where, his sister-in-law told him, the young giants kept their hearts. He then gouged out their eyes and threw them into the fire, putting one in each of the four corners.

The giant's wife crushed the obsidian as her brother-in-law had told her, and placed it on a deer hide. Then Chipmunk's brother told her to start for home. He warned her especially not to lose the obsidian.

"If they catch you," he said, "you can use it. Throw it in their eyes."

Following his advice she started. He, meanwhile, proceeded to dig holes, one toward the south, one toward the east, one toward the north, and one toward the west, so that he might conceal himself and dodge from one to the other in case he were pursued by the giant. He made holes all around the house, both inside and outside. After he had finished digging the holes he thought about the giant and wondered when he would return. He went into the hills, cut a hard manzanita stick, and sharpened one edge of it.

Then he walked around. Soon the giant appeared, coming over the hill. As he approached the house, Chipmunk's brother stepped inside.

The giant saw him and said to himself: "There is another victim." He was glad that he had another person to kill, and he followed close behind him into the house.

Chipmunk's brother now asked the giant, "What do you do first, when you come home?"

The giant replied, "I dance. Just watch me dance."

Then Chipmunk's brother went into the holes he had dug and came forth in different places. The giant tried to catch him and followed him about, but Chipmunk's brother was too quick for him and dodged into the holes. The giant chased him around the house. Every time that the giant neared him, he jumped into a hole, appearing again in another part of the house.

He told the giant, "You cannot catch me unless you dance. After you dance, I will let you catch me. I want to see you dance first."

Chipmunk's brother stayed outside, while the giant danced. He shouted at the giant and said, "Dance more. Jump higher through that smoke hole. I like to see you dance." The giant did as Chipmunk's brother told him. While he danced, Chipmunk's brother with his manzanita stick climbed on top of the house. Suddenly he struck the giant across the neck, chopping his head off with the sharp stick. The head rolled down close to the spring near the house and the body of the giant collapsed inside of the house.

But the giant had many brothers, and they also dreamt of their brother one day. So they all set out for his house. Arrived there they perceived meat scattered about on the rocks and trees. They did not know that this was their brother, whom Chipmunk's brother had cut up after killing, and scattered around. So they set to and cooked and ate this meat, thinking it to be some of their brother's victims. The youngest giant, having eaten all he could, went to the spring to drink, and there discovered the giant's head where it had rolled after Chipmunk's brother cut it off. Then they knew that they had eaten their own brother.

"Who could have killed him?" they cried.

They decided to sleep and see whether they would dream about it.

It was the youngest brother's dreams that set them off in pursuit of Chipmunk's widow. Many times they overtook her, only to have her escape when she blinded them by throwing the crushed obsidian in their eyes. By the time they had picked it out of their eyes, she was far ahead of them.

At last Chipmunk's widow reached the house of her father, Lizard. Once she was safely within his doors, with the giants in hot pursuit, Lizard spat on the house and turned it to stone.

Then Lizard called upon the wind to destroy the giant's brothers, but they blew the wind back. Lizard next called upon the snow for aid, but the giants melted the snow by shouting, and when the hail was summoned they stopped the hail by shouting. But at last Lizard called upon the flood, which succeeded in drowning them.

Thus came to an end Yayali, the giant, and his many brothers.

The Skyland

The Skyland

HOW ROUGH-NOSE SAVED HIS BROTHER
[As told by the Hupa indians of Humboldt county]

Rough-Nose and his younger brother lived together. While Rough-Nose hunted for deer his brother remained at home roasting the meat. He had been told many times by his elder brother not, under any circumstances, to roast the short ribs of the deer. One day when Rough-Nose was away hunting, the younger brother got to thinking about it.

"Why does he always tell me that?" he said to himself. "I shall roast them this time."

But when he had roasted them "something" carried him off. When Rough-Nose arrived home from the hunt he could not find his younger brother. He looked everywhere for him.

Then he knew. "He must have roasted the short ribs," he said, and began to cry.

Day after day he would sit out in the clearing in the forest with his cane sticking up beside him, and mourn for his brother. And always a bird came and alighted on the cane and said, "His brother has been carried off. His brother has been carried off."

After several days of this, it began to annoy Rough-Nose.

"I wish I could do something to him. If I could catch him I'd kill him," he said.

So the next day when he went out to sit down he put

pitch on the top of his cane. The bird came and lit on
it as usual and was easily caught.

"Now I will kill you," he said.

"Don't kill me," said the bird, "I will tell you where
they have taken your brother. They are roasting him in
the world above. Gather some people and have them
make rope. With the help of that you can go there. I
will go ahead of you."

Rough-Nose then called the people he wanted –
Spider and Coyote to make rope, with which to climb
to the world above, Caterpillar to make the trail,
Mouse to chew off the bowstrings of the people in the
world above, Frog to put out the fires, and Louse to tie
together the enemy by their hair as they slept.

Coyote and Spider commenced to make the rope.
Coyote soon had a storage basket full, but Spider's rope
was fine, and looked like only one coil. Coyote made
fun of it saying, "That looks as if it would reach a long
way." But when it came to tying the rope to an arrow
and shooting it upwards to see if it was long enough to
reach the world above, Coyote's rope fell back. Spider's
went up until it could be seen no longer, and finally
they heard the arrow, to which Spider's rope was tied,
strike the sky with a ringing noise.

Then Caterpillar went ahead, made the trail, and
returned.

Rough-Nose next caught a woodrat, placed it in his
sack, and with the rest of the people started up the trail
made by Caterpillar to the world above. At the top
he said, "You wait here. I will go along to the place
where the fire is – where they are roasting my brother."

He changed himself into an old woman and walked
with a widow's cane.

He came up to the fire and said to the old woman tending it, "May I warm myself by your fire?"

"You might be Rough-Nose," said the old woman.

"Oh, yes, that fellow is likely to come here," said Rough-Nose, "but I am not he."

The old woman made no reply, but commenced poking the bag in which the boy was hanging over the fire. Rough-Nose waited until he heard all the other people of the sky world eating in the house near-by. Then he caught the old woman and held her in the fire until she was dead. He stripped her clothes off and dressed himself in them. Then he went over to the sack, took his younger brother out, and put the woodrat in his place.

At that moment, someone put his head out of the house, and called, "Come and eat."

Rough-Nose answered, "Just throw something out here for me."

When the people had gone to bed Rough-Nose and his companions made an attack on them. Frog put the fires out, causing complete darkness; Mouse chewed off the bowstrings of the enemy; and Louse tied together their hair. All was confusion. Cries of "My hair hurts," and "A mouse has chewed my bowstring," could be heard from the people in the dark. Others ran and jumped into their canoes to give chase, but they filled with water and sank. The mice had gnawed holes in them.

Then Rough-Nose, carrying his brother, went safely home.

THE LOST BROTHER
[As told by the northern Yana indians of Shasta county]

Pine Marten had a younger brother called Weasel. One day he left Weasel at home while he went hunting. He cautioned him, however, to hide. So Weasel hid himself under the edge of the roof.

A little time passed and then Lizard strolled in. Weasel peeped out and saw him. He thought him very handsome and so decided to come out and play with him. He offered Lizard fat to eat, and as Lizard ate and ate he grew bigger and bigger. This scared Weasel, who began to cry. Then Lizard picked up Weasel and carried him off.

When Pine Marten came home from the hunt there was no sign of his younger brother. He asked everyone if they knew where his brother had vanished to, but nobody knew.

Pine Marten then set out to seek his brother. He used Mouse's very long arrow of tules to climb to the sky. Once there he directed his steps to the east. On the way he met Moon, who had come from the east and was traveling toward the west.

"I came to ask you something, for living up here you ought to see everything. Have you seen my brother?"

"Yes," replied Moon. "See over there (and he pointed down to the earth and a long distance from Pine Marten's house), your brother is being hung up over the fire by Lizard. The Lizard people are going to roast him."

Moon told Pine Marten to go back to the earth and directed him how to reach his brother.

"What can I give you to show my appreciation of

your aid?" asked Pine Marten of Moon. "Will you
have red and blue beads?"

"Yes," said Moon.

Pine Marten gave the beads to him, and we now see
them as a halo around the moon.

Pine Marten then returned to earth and in company
with Coyote, who had turned himself into an old woman, set out for the place where Moon had shown him
his brother was being prepared for roasting over the
fire. When they neared the fire Coyote went ahead by
himself and approached Lizard.

"I am your aunt," he said to Lizard. "I hear you
stole Pine Marten's brother and are going to kill him."

Lizard eyed the old woman with suspicion.

"You are Coyote. You are trying to fool me," he
said.

"No, I'm not Coyote. I'm your old aunt," Coyote
answered.

Lizard then believed him.

Far off, hidden from sight, was Pine Marten, watching. He blew toward Lizard, making it seem very
cold, and then he said, "Be heavy."

"I'm cold. I'm going to get warm," said Lizard as
the cold sent by Pine Marten blew around him.

He tried to lift a load of wood to carry over to the
fire, but when Pine Marten had blown the cold over
and called out "Be heavy," this firewood had then become very heavy. It was too heavy for him to carry,
now. Coyote offered to push it up on his back. So he
came up behind Lizard, but, instead of assisting, as he
said he would, he gave the ground a great kick; it
opened and Lizard and his load went down out of
sight.

Pine Marten came running up at this point. He dug Lizard up out of the ground, skinned him, and put on his hide. When he entered Lizard's house, where he knew his brother was tied up ready to be killed that night, the people looked suspiciously at him.

"That must be a stranger," they said. They all got up and began to cry out.

Pine Marten whipped them and they all became quiet. When night came he gathered all the Lizard people together for a big sweat dance.

"Let us dance," he said, "and then we will sleep."

They did so. After the dance Pine Marten blew deeply and all the people fell into a sound sleep. Then he untied his brother and brought him away with him. Before he left, however, he covered the house with pitch inside and out, and set fire to it. All the people were burned, and Pine Marten returned home with his lost brother.

KIDNAPPED IN SKYLAND
[As told by the central Miwok indians of Tuolumne county]

One day Salamander came to Chipmunk and said, "I saw a big deer but I could not kill him. I tried to break his neck, but I could not and he escaped from me."

Chipmunk answered, "My father is lost because of Salamander's troubles."

Chipmunk started out then to seek his lost father. After a long time he found some of his father's tracks and followed them. He came to a creek, but after crossing it he lost sight of the tracks and started again to hunt for them. A little way up the creek he saw a large deer and he followed it for a long way.

Suddenly he saw two women approaching. He stopped quickly in his tracks and was about to leave the trail. Then he changed his mind and kept on.

One of the women said, "Let us catch him. He is going to pass near us. We will not let him pass."

"Get away, please," Chipmunk said. "I am searching for my father."

He tried very hard to push the two women from the path, but they would not move. He tried to pass between them, but they would not leave the trail. Then they caught hold of him. They called up to their father.

"Father, we have got a man who is looking for his father. He has been searching and has not had anything to eat for ten days."

Their father came to help them take their prisoner home.

"Keep your father away from me," Chipmunk said. "I don't want him to come near me."

All the while Chipmunk was thinking, "This is what must have happened to my father."

Chipmunk did not know who the girls were or where they were taking him. He thought it was to be his last time on earth. The two women tied Chipmunk with a rope and carried him up into the sky. They wanted to marry him.

"I don't know if anyone will find me," he said. "It is Salamander's fault that I am caught. If I escape I shall even the score with him."

But he did not know how to escape. When he arrived in the sky he found that all the people were Deer people. The two Deer women wanted to fatten Chipmunk before they married him. So they cooked many seeds to feed him, but he did not want them. "Take it away from me. Do not place it near me," said Chipmunk, for the seeds did not smell good to him. In despair the girls said to each other, "I don't know what he likes to eat."

Then Chipmunk said, "You girls might just as well let me eat your father. I am getting hungry and I shall eat him. There is no use trying to save him. The old man is pretty poor, but I shall eat him just the same." "Our father is across the way," said the girls.

"Let me see how I can shoot him with my bow and arrow," said Chipmunk.

Then he began to sing, and old Deer became fat. He became so fat that he could not walk. Then Chipmunk took one arrow and shot the old Deer and killed him.

"I don't know where I shall go after I have eaten Deer," said Chipmunk to himself. "If I don't leave this place I think I must kill more, but I shall do my best to leave this place."

Meanwhile Chipmunk's older brother was searching for him.

"I don't know what has happened to my brother," he said. "I find him nowhere."

At last he arrived at the place where the Deer women had captured Chipmunk. His leg became entangled in some rope which they had dropped when they tied Chipmunk. He knew then what had happened to his brother, and he cried and cried.

"I fear they killed my brother after they took him up there," he said. "I shall try to climb somehow and if I reach that place I will put the Deer to sleep."

All night long he climbed until he finally arrived in the sky, where his brother was. He started to cry when he saw him and knew that he was safe.

"Don't cry any more," Chipmunk said, "for I am still safe."

Then Chipmunk's brother began to sing and thus put the Deer people to sleep.

When the people were asleep he said to Chipmunk, "Get ready. We are going home."

Chipmunk got ready and then his brother said, "You get on one end of this arrow."

As soon as Chipmunk was on the end of the arrow his brother shot it straight down to their home. Then he got on another and sailed down, too.

Thus he brought his brother back from Skyland.

"You had better stay home," he said to him then. "Never hunt again and don't go into the hills. They might catch you again."

"I was caught because of Salamander," Chipmunk said. "All of this trouble is his fault. I will have revenge upon him."

When he entered his house he saw Salamander lying beside the fire.

"I shall kill you," he said to him. "I shall throw you into the fire. You might just as well take your last breath now. You are the fellow who deceived me. You told me that you saw large deer."

Then he threw Salamander into the fire. And thus Chipmunk got his revenge.

Star Stories

Star Stories

THE PLEIADES

[As told by the Tachi indians of Kings county]

A long time ago five girls lived in the sky. They sang and played all night in the sky.

There was only one man whom they liked, and he was Flea. So they all married him and he went everywhere with them. One summer Flea became sick with the itch. This caused his wives to dislike him.

"Let us run away," they said. "Where shall we go?" They agreed to go east.

"When shall we go?" they said.

"As soon as he sleeps," one of them answered.

So when Flea went to sleep, his five wives got up and went off and left him. They had gone far away when Flea awoke.

"Where are my wives?" he said.

He soon discovered that they had gone away.

"Where shall I go?" he asked, and then decided to go east.

At last he came in sight of them.

"I will catch you," he said.

"He is coming. Let us run," the women said.

So they started to run.

"Do you see him again?" one asked.

"Yes, he is near," another replied.

"Let us go up into the air. Then he cannot come with us," they said.

So they rose up, but Flea rose, too.

They can all be seen now in the sky as stars. The five women are close together in the Pleiades and Flea is the star at the side of them.

THE PLEIADES
[As told by the Shasta indians of Siskiyou county]

One day, Coyote and Raccoon were returning together from a dance. Along the road they noticed a hole, and a little farther on another hole. A squirrel ran into one of the holes as they passed by.

"You stop him from coming out of the other hole," said Coyote to Raccoon.

"All right," Raccoon replied, and he put his hand in the other hole to scare the squirrel and so make him turn back and try to escape through the opening by which he had entered.

Coyote at his end put his hand in, and seized something.

"Look out, you have hold of me," cried Raccoon.

"No," said Coyote, "that is the squirrel."

"No, that is I," answered Raccoon. "I tell you that is I."

"No," answered Coyote, "that is the squirrel."

So Coyote kept on pulling until he pulled off Raccoon's arm and killed him. Then Coyote went home. He told his children to go and bring in what he had killed. They went and returned with all of Raccoon's body and ate it, but they did not give any share to their youngest brother.

This made the little fellow very angry, and so he went to Raccoon's children and said: "Coyote has killed your father."

Raccoon's children thanked this youngest Coyote and told him to return home. The next day, while Coyote was away, Raccoon's children came to Coyote's house and killed all his children except the youngest. They carried off this one child with them, and went up into the sky.

When Coyote returned and found no children, he cried: "I don't know where they are."

He ran through all the house. Then he went to Raccoon's house, but there were no children there. Then he noticed the dust rising in eddies. He looked up and saw Raccoon's children and his youngest rising. He ran after them but could not catch them.

Raccoon's children became the Pleiades. (Coyote's youngest child is the small star near the Pleiades.) In winter, when raccoons are in their holes, the Pleiades are most brilliant, and continually visible. In summer, when raccoons are out and about, the Pleiades are not seen.

WHENCE SOME STARS CAME
[As told by the Cahuilla indians of Riverside county]

Once there lived three little girls, Moki, Kipi, and Tewe. They were very small and not at all pretty, but were always laughing. They used to wonder why Tukwishhemish, who was a very pretty woman, never opened her mouth when she laughed. But one day, when they had made her laugh very hard, she opened her mouth, and then they saw that, instead of having one row of teeth, she had two. The little girls thought this very funny, and they laughed at her.

Tukwishhemish was so ashamed that she went up to the sky and became a star. Soon the little girls became lonely and they, too, went to the sky and became stars.

Far away, however, two brothers who had heard of these girls decided to make them their wives.

When they arrived at the home of the girls and found that they had left they felt very badly. They set out and traveled all over the world looking for them, but of course could not find them.

One night while sleeping in a house one of the brothers awoke. He lay and gazed out of the smoke-hole. He saw the stars in the sky and knew that they were the little girls. He wondered how he could get to them. At last he thought of a way. He took a stick and put it into the fire until it began to burn. Then he shot it up through the smoke-hole and it went to the sky. He followed this path and reached the sky and became a star.

After a while the other brother awoke and missed his partner. He wondered where he had gone. So the following night he slept in his brother's place. When he awoke in the night he, too, saw the little girl stars in the sky, and then he knew where his brother had gone.

He did the same thing as his brother and reached the sky and became a star.

And there the two brother stars remain, guarding the little girl stars.

THE MAGICIAN AND HIS SON
[As told by the Cahuilla indians of Riverside county]

Once upon a time there lived a very powerful magician named Tukvachtahat. His wife and son, who was named Kunvachmal, lived with him, but the magician was always quarreling with his wife. Finally they separated, Kunvachmal remaining with his mother.

It was not long before Tukvachtahat married again

and had two sons by this marriage. Tukvachtahat was
a very rich man and his family had everything they
wanted. But Kunvachmal and his mother were very
poor.

One day Kunvachmal visited his half-brothers and
saw the fine things they had. He was jealous, and when
he went home he told his mother that he wanted fine
things like his half-brothers had. His mother replied
that they were poor and could not have such fine things.

Kunvachmal started to cry at this, so his mother went
outside and made him a bow and arrow of mesquite
wood. When Kunvachmal called upon his half-brothers again he showed them his bow and arrows. They
took his arrows and broke them. At this Kunvachmal
cried and went home and told his mother what had
happened. She told him not to go back anymore, but
Kunvachmal did not listen, and each day he returned
only to have his arrows broken.

Finally, however, the brothers tired of breaking his
arrows, and they decided to play a game with him by
which they thought they could win the arrows and keep
them for themselves, instead of breaking them, for they
were beautifully-made arrows.

At first they won, and each day Kunvachmal went
home without any arrows. Soon he began to win, however, and took home the fine arrows belonging to his
brothers. This made them angry and they told their
father how things were going. Tukvachtahat did not
like this at all and told his boys they must get even with
Kunvachmal. He told them to have a race to the water
next day to go swimming, but to let Kunvachmal win
and dive in. The water looked like a small pool, but he
told them that in reality it was the ocean.

So the next day the brothers suggested to Kunvachmal that they have a race to the water and that the first one there should dive in. They took off their clothes and started, but as agreed between the two brothers, Kunvachmal won and dived in. He sank clear to the bottom and, since it was the ocean, it was very deep. But he did not drown, as his brothers had expected, for Kunvachmal, unknown even to himself, had a great deal of magical power like his father. He sat down at the bottom of the ocean and wondered what he could do to get out. He turned into a frog and swam to the top of the water. Then he turned himself into a water-ant and got out. He arrived home and found his mother crying. She had cried all night and all day, while he had been gone. So he dried her tears, and they were happy again. But when Tukvachtahat heard no more crying he knew that Kunvachmal had outwitted him, and he was very angry, indeed. He planned again to get rid of Kunvachmal.

This time the three brothers went hunting for rabbits. They built fires and started to drive the rabbits. After some rabbits had been trapped this way Kunvachmal began killing them. While he was busy thus his brothers caused the fires to surround him, hoping to burn him to death. Kunvachmal soon realized his danger. He began to sing, and at the same time sank down into the ground, so that by the time the fires had come together he was under the earth and safe. When the fire had gone out he waited for the ground to cool and then came up and went home. His mother was overjoyed to see him and she stopped crying. Then again Tukvachtahat knew that Kunvachmal had gotten the best of him.

One day Kunvachmal saw Tukvachtahat plant

wheat. He stole a few grains out of his father's sack and sowed it in the mountains. His brothers saw him do this and they told their father about it. Tukvachtahat was so angry that he caused it to rain hard and wash all of Kunvachmal's wheat away. Kunvachmal, in revenge, sang his song and made it rain still harder and made the wind blow so as to carry his father's wheat away also.

Then he told the birds and insects to gather the wheat which had been washed out of his father's ground and bring it to him, so he could store it away. Because of this, Kunvachmal became very rich and Tukvachtahat poor. The time came when Tukvachtahat came to Kunvachmal and begged for food, that he and his sons might eat, for they were starving.

Kunvachmal said, "Surely, go help yourself."

Later on, a big feast was being held some distance away. Tukvachtahat and his sons were invited to attend and sing. Kunvachmal wanted to go also, but his mother said no, for he did not have fine enough clothes and could not sing well.

Kunvachmal did not listen to his mother and went to the feast. No one paid any attention to him, for he was too poorly dressed. This made him feel badly and he decided to go into a hole and get clothes made of the colors which are on a worm. Then he got the mosquitoes to sing for him. When he returned to the feast everyone stopped admiring his father and brothers to gaze at him. His clothes far surpassed those of any of the other guests and his singing was beautiful.

When Kunvachmal returned from the feast he was very happy. After a while he went to the sky and became a bright star. This star comes up at night just over the horizon for a little while and then goes right back again.

[Wheat was not cultivated until after the coming of Caucasians, so that the episode concerning wheat is a modern addition to the story.]

Thunder

Thunder

THE THUNDER DOG
[As told by the Yana indians of Shasta county]

One day Flint Boy dreamed of a beautiful woman, who lived with her father, Chiuchiuwayu, in the Yallo Bally mountains.

"I want to go there," he said to his grandmother. "I am going to marry this beautiful woman."

His grandmother looked at him.

"Yes," she said.

"But I want someone for company on the road," Flint Boy said. "I want some one who makes a lot of noise. He must speak a different language."

"How do you want him to talk?" his grandmother asked. "What do you want him to say?"

"When he sees any one coming I want him to say 'Wu! Wu!' like a dog."

Then they dug up someone from the ground. Flint Boy asked him to bark and when he did so everyone heard the noise all over the world. They knew it was Flint Boy's dog. So now Flint Boy set out with his dog for Yallo Bally mountain, the home of the girl he had dreamed about. When he arrived at the house of the girl he made his dog remain outside.

"I am going to marry the girl. When I have done so I shall get up early to hunt, and I shall tell her to take care of you."

He then entered the house. Many people were there.

He went over and sat down by the girl. Everyone looked at him. The girl's father said to her, "Where did that man come from?"

The girl said she did not know.

"It looks as though you were married," said her father, so he gave her a black bearskin for Flint Boy to sit on.

Flint Boy married the girl. Early the next morning he got up and told his wife about the dog. He told her that it was vicious and that she must not touch it, or talk to it, for it would bite her.

"Just leave him alone where he is," he said.

She agreed to care for it. So Flint Boy went away to hunt.

When he was far away his wife went out to look at the dog. She patted it, saying, "Nice dog."

The dog shook his head and tail, and said, "Where is my master?"

She answered, "He has gone away."

At this the dog barked. He did not want to be tied up. He wanted to go with Flint Boy on his hunt. He barked so loudly that everyone heard it all over the world, and all were terribly frightened. Far away Flint Boy heard it. He knew that someone had touched his dog and he feared that perhaps they had turned him loose.

"I believe I've lost my dog," he said.

He returned home. His wife met him and said, "I've fed him and turned him loose."

"He's a vicious dog. You ought not to have touched him," he told her.

That night it grew cloudy. On top of Yallo Bally mountain there was a great cloud, black and thick.

Flint Boy's dog had called it to come and roll him up in it and take him up in the air. The cloud came down over the dog; it swirled and rolled, and it went up in the air with him. Half way up the dog barked and all over the world he was heard.

Flint Boy heard it and was sad, for he knew the dog was lost. Flint Boy's dog had gone to live in the black clouds, and now when he barks it thunders all over the world and then the dog sends down the rain.

THE BEGINNING OF THUNDER
[As told by the central Miwok indians of Tuolumne county]

Bear's sister-in-law, Deer, had two beautiful daughters, called Fawns. Bear was a horrible, wicked woman, and she wanted the Fawns for herself. So this is what she did.

One day she invited Deer to accompany her when she went to pick clover. The two Fawns remained at home. While resting during the day, after having picked much clover, Bear offered to pick out lice from Deer's head. While doing so she watched her chance, took Deer unaware, and bit her neck so hard that she killed her. Then she devoured her, all excepting the liver. This she placed in the bottom of a basket filled with clover, and took it home. She gave the basket of clover to the Fawns to eat.

When they asked where their mother was, she replied, "She will come soon. You know she is always slow and takes her time in coming home."

So the Fawns ate the clover, but when they reached the bottom of the basket, they discovered the liver. Then they knew that their aunt had killed their mother.

"We had better watch out, or she will kill us too," they said to one another. They decided to leave without saying anything and go to their grandfather. So the next day when Bear was away they got together all the baskets and awls which belonged to Deer and departed. They left one basket, however, in the house.

When Bear returned and found the Fawns missing she hunted for their tracks and set out after them. After she had tracked them a short distance, the basket, left at home, whistled. Bear ran back to the house, thinking the Fawns had returned. But she could not find them and so set out again, following their tracks.

The Fawns, meanwhile, had proceeded on their journey, throwing awls and baskets in different directions. These awls and baskets whistled. Each time Bear thought that the Fawns were whistling, and left the trail in search of them. And each time that Bear was fooled in this manner, she became angrier and angrier.

She shouted in her anger. "Those girls are making a fool of me. When I capture them I'll eat them."

The awls only whistled in response and Bear ran toward the sound. There was no one there.

Finally, the Fawns, far ahead of Bear, came to the river. On the opposite side they saw Daddy Longlegs. They asked him to stretch his leg across the river so that they might cross safely. They told him that Bear had killed their mother and they were fleeing from her. So when Bear at last came to the river, Daddy Longlegs stretched his leg over again, but when the wicked aunt of the two Fawns, walking on his leg, reached the middle of the river, Daddy Longlegs gave a sudden jump and threw her into the river. But Bear did not drown.

She managed to swim to the shore, where she again started in pursuit of the Fawns. But the Fawns were far ahead of their aunt, and soon reached their grandfather's house. Their grandfather was Lizard. They told him of the terrible fate which had overtaken their mother.

"Where is Bear?" he asked them.

"She is following us and will soon be here," they replied. Upon hearing this Lizard threw two large white stones into the fire and heated them. When Bear arrived outside of Lizard's house she could not find an entrance. She asked Lizard how she should enter, and he told her that the only entrance was through the smokehole, so she must climb on the roof and enter that way. He also told her that when she entered she must close her eyes tightly and open wide her mouth. Bear did as she was instructed, for she was very anxious to get the two Fawns, whom Lizard had told her were in his house. But as Bear entered, eyes closed and mouth open, Lizard took the red hot stones from the fire and thrust them down her throat. Bear rolled from the top of Lizard's house dead.

Lizard then skinned her and dressed her hide, after which he cut it in two pieces, one large and one small. The larger piece he gave to the older Fawn, the smaller piece to the younger. Then Lizard instructed the girls to run about and see what kind of noise was made by Bear's skin. The girls proceeded to run around, the skins making all kinds of loud noises. Lizard, watching them, laughed and said to himself, "The girls are all right. They are Thunders. I think I had better send them up to the sky."

When the Fawns came to Lizard to tell him that

they were going to return home, he said, "Do not go home. I have a good place for you. I shall send you to the sky."

So the girls went up to the sky. There Lizard could hear them running about. Their aunt's skin, which they had kept, makes the loud noises, that we call thunder. When the Fawn girls ran around in the sky Rain and Hail fell.

So now whenever the girls (Thunders, as Lizard called them) run around above, rain begins to fall.

THUNDER
[As told by the Nisenan indians of Sacramento county]

There once lived a man who did not eat the food of this earth. Only the food of the sky did he eat. When he wanted to eat he would speak in spirit language and then acorn bread would come down. This man had two grandsons, orphans, whom he took care of. The boys often wondered how their grandfather fed, since he did not touch the food which they ate. One day they followed him as he left the house, and saw where and how he obtained his bread. As quickly as he ate the bread more appeared. There was no end to it. They approached their grandfather and asked him for some of the food. He gave them a very little, saying that it was enough.

"It is the best that we have ever eaten," they said to him.

"You have plenty of other food; don't touch this," their grandfather said.

But as they went away to play with their hoop they said: "We will eat some more when he is gone."

They played with their hoop for a long time, and
when they at last came in the old man was not there.
They immediately went to the bread and helped themselves. But it did not replenish as it had before, and
when their grandfather returned there was very little
bread left. He knew what they had done and resolved
to punish them.

He called them, gave them arrows, and told them to
shoot a flicker. When they brought it in, he divided the
feathers, those of the right wing to the older, of the left
to the younger; the tail he split, six feathers to each.
Then he made them headbands, put them on them,
tightened their belts, and sent them out to play with
their hoop. But he had given their hoop instructions to
lead them to a good place to live.

So when the boys threw their hoop it rolled away.
They ran after it but could not overtake it. When they
ran it rolled fast; when they walked it rolled slowly.
It was always just out of reach. It led them far away
and up a high mountain, and then stopped.

The younger brother saw what was happening, and
he cried:

"Dear brother, it is taking us away."

Then the boys took off their belts, made them into
slings with which they threw a stone up in the air,
breaking the sky open. The hoop started to roll up,
taking the boys with it into the sky. Back at home the
old man heard them, like thunder on the highest mountain.

"Now they are in a good place where there is no
trouble, and there is better food than here," he said.

It is thunder when the boys roll their hoop.

THUNDER'S DAUGHTER

[As told by the northeastern Maidu indians of Plumas county]

Thunder had a very beautiful daughter who went about luring young men to destruction. By inducing them to follow her she got them into situations where, without the magic which she possessed, they could not meet the obstacles that confronted them, and so always met death.

One day Thunder's daughter passed the home of two brothers. Upon seeing such a beautiful woman, the elder brother, Pitmulussi, said: "I am going to follow her."

"No, she is no good," his mother and father said. They tried to dissuade him, but to no avail.

So this brother set out. He took an arrow and shot it so that it fell ahead of the girl and stuck in the ground. Thunder's daughter had a basket filled with ice on her back. She picked up the arrow and put it into this basket, and said: "I think I shall have an arrow to take to my father."

Now it was up to Pitmulussi to get it out of the basket, otherwise he would die. After shooting the arrow Pitmulussi ran very quickly after the girl and caught up with her. He put his hand underneath the basket, and managed to pull his arrow out. Thus he got the best of the girl. But Thunder, who was watching, called out: "Some one has the best of us." As he spoke it thundered all over the world.

By and by Thunder's daughter came to a large patch of wild roses. They had grown very thickly and had many thorns. They parted immediately, however, as she walked through them, and then closed up behind her and left no trace of a path.

Pitmulussi, however, had taken with him a piece of flint, and placing it on the ground, he said: "You must cut me a path." Working from side to side, the piece of flint cut a pathway, through which he followed the girl. Again Thunder saw and screamed out a warning, and again it thundered all over.

Next, Thunder's daughter came to a place where there were a great number of rattlesnakes, and by the aid of her magic passed through them all safely. Pitmulussi, close behind, stopped and put on his stone moccasins. These moccasins reached up to his waist, and were red hot, and so he was able to walk through the snakes in safety. Then it thundered, for again Thunder was calling out to his daughter.

Still Thunder's daughter went on, besetting Pitmulussi's path with many dangers. But Pitmulussi cared not, for he knew that if he could overcome all these dangers he would win the girl for his wife. She brought Pitmulussi to a great river, covered with ice so slippery that no one could stand on it. She passed over easily, however. When Pitmulussi came up he again put on his red hot moccasins, and with these walked over easily, melting the ice. Again it thundered.

Next the girl led him through the valley of Old Age. In this valley people died of old age before they could pass through. Pitmulussi traveled and traveled, following the girl, till it seemed as if he never would get through. He began to grow gray, then white, and finally became very weak. Then his spirit helpers said to him: "Stick the feather of the Atataim bird in your hair."

He did so, and he became young again, and was able to reach the other end of the valley.

Beyond this valley of Old Age was a great sweat-house, all of solid ice, in which Thunder lived. Thunder's daughter reached the sweathouse and walked up the outside to the top, entering through the smokehole. When Pitmulussi reached the house he put on his stone moccasins, and walking easily up the outside of the house, entered through the smokehole and sat down beside Thunder's daughter.

Thunder roared at him, and all over the world people heard. Thunder gave Pitmulussi many tasks to do, hoping to destroy him, but Pitmulussi's spirits helped him each time, and finally Thunder gave in and allowed Pitmulussi to take his daughter and return to his home.

Adventure Stories

Adventure Stories

THE CONQUEROR

[As told by the northeastern Maidu indians of Plumas county]

There were a lot of wicked people in the world a long time ago, and they were gradually killing everybody. After a while there were only three people left, two old men who had managed to escape being killed, and their one daughter. One day while the daughter was picking clover a man came to her.

"I am Cloud-Man," he said. "I live far up in the sky. If you will marry me I will give you two children."

The daughter assented and so the Cloud-Man stayed and talked to her for a long time. Before he left he gave her two bunches of black feathers.

"These will be our children," he said. "One will be Always-Eating, the other will be Conqueror."

When the two old men discovered the two boys they asked, "Where did these boys come from? We never saw them before."

The boys' mother answered, "Can't you be sensible? When you see something which you don't understand why don't you let it alone?"

Soon after the boys went outside. From off a bluff they heard Ground Squirrel calling, "Titsuk, titsuk, titsuk."

Conqueror returned to the house and spoke to his grandfathers.

"Give me your bow and arrows. I want to go and kill Ground Squirrel."

"No," the old men said. "The bluff where Ground Squirrel lives is one of the places where so many of our people were killed. Some wicked people live there, and Ground Squirrel is only calling to you so that these people may kill you when you reach his house. That is the way so many of our people were killed before you came. Let Ground Squirrel alone; let him bark."

But Conqueror answered, "I want to try, anyhow. Give me the bow and arrows."

So the old men gave him the bow and arrows.

Conqueror stood in the doorway of the house and shot at Ground Squirrel. He killed him. Then he put on a pair of stone shoes and went over to the bluff where Ground Squirrel lay, dead. As he approached he saw all around the bones of those who had been killed. He had no sooner reached the body of Ground Squirrel when from all around rattlesnakes began to come out. They surrounded him and began to strike at him. But Conqueror stamped on them with his stone shoes and killed them. Then he pulled up the rocks and pulled out all the snakes that were under them, stamped on them, and killed them all. So it was that Conqueror killed the rattlesnakes, and also Ground Squirrel, the wicked person who lured people from their homes to the bluff where he lived and where they met death from the rattlesnakes.

That night as Conqueror stood outside of his house he heard a sound as of people dancing. He went in and told his people that he was going to see what it was.

"No, you must not go," said his grandfathers. "They are Wood-Bug's people, and they are another wicked people who have been the cause of so many deaths amongst our people. Stay here. Do not go, for they will kill you, too."

But Conqueror would not heed his grandfathers. Putting on his shirt of red-hot rock he went to the place whence the sound of dancing had come.

Wood-Bug met him at the door and said, "Come in and dance."

So Conqueror entered and started dancing. The people began to knock him about, for this was what they had done to his relatives, and had killed them that way. But Conqueror did the same to them. He knocked them this way and that, and burned them with his red-hot stone shirt, thus killing them all. So Conqueror overcame all these people and killed them. When he told his grandfathers they were glad, for Wood-Bug and his people had killed a great many of their people by knocking them around.

Next morning Conqueror set off to another place, where lived a wicked woman, called Man-Straightening-Old-Woman. She, too, had killed many of his relatives. As he approached her house she eyed him up and down, approvingly.

"What a fine-looking man you are!" she called out to him. "Only you are not straight. If your back were straight you would look better."

Then she brought out a flat, long stone, and showed it to Conqueror.

"Let me take this and straighten you out – straighten your arms, legs, and body – and then when I get done you will be a straight man."

Conqueror went inside the house and she made him lie down on his stomach on a bed of stone. Then she started to rub him with the stone in her hand. Behind her, however, she had a large stone, and it was her intention, as she had done with many of Conqueror's relatives, to take this stone and hit him in the small of his back, while he lay there, and thus kill him. As she struck at Conqueror with the stone he dodged and jumped off the bed, and she missed. She hit the rock on which he had been lying, and a piece flew off and killed her. Conqueror then went home, glad that he had killed this wicked woman.

Then one day he said to his grandfathers, "Did you ever go anywhere to gamble? If you did, let us go and gamble."

"We used to gamble at Helaiono," they said, "but that is where we lost many of our people."

Conqueror, however, wanted to go and so the next morning they set out. They traveled a long distance, and finally reached a river, in the middle of which was a plant sticking up out of the water.

"We used to swim across at this place," they told Conqueror. "We had to swim far away from that plant in order to arrive at the other side safely . Many times someone would swim too near the plant and then it would pull them far down and they would drown."

"Let us try it, one at a time," said Conqueror. "You go first, for I want to see how you do it."

So they swam, one after the other. But when Conqueror went he swam up to the plant, pulled it up, and carried it with him to the other side.

There they were met by the people of the place, who invited them into their dance house to gamble.

The grandfathers told Conqueror that the floor in this dance house was of ice and that it sloped down steeply. Here, many of Conqueror's relatives, they told him, had met death, for when they tried to walk on this floor they slipped, fell, and slid about until they got killed.

Conqueror then put on his stone shoes and went in. He crushed the floor as he stepped on it and broke it all to pieces.

Then they started to gamble with these people.

The other side won first, and they took an eye from each of the old men. This was their way of gambling.

Then they played again and the two old men won their eyes back.

The person gambling with Conqueror had a path through his body, and could pass the gambling bones through this from one hand to the other. He kept winning because of this. After awhile Conqueror caught on and he stopped up this passage in his opponent's body without being seen. Then he opened a pathway in his own body, and so began to win.

While he played he sang the song that North Wind sings, and in this way called North Wind to him. When North Wind came he froze up everything and thus killed the people.

Conqueror and his grandfathers returned home, for they had conquered all the wicked people who had caused the death of their relatives.

THE AVENGER OF THE CUPEÑO
[As told by the Cupeño indians of San Diego county]

Long ago the Cupeño lived in the north, but they left and came to Kupa to settle because the sun always shone there. They brought with them a green, hair-like water plant as their hot water supply. Wherever they placed this plant they had springs of boiling water. Then one day the Cupeño were attacked by their enemies, who surprised them, clubbed them to death, and burned their homes. Only one woman and her infant son escaped the massacre. This woman was hiding in her house with her baby boy when the attackers set fire to it. Upon seeing her they called to her to come out of her burning house. She appeared with the baby in her arms. She told them the infant was a girl, and therefore they spared mother and child. The child's name was Hoboyak, which means "Able to do anything." Hoboyak's mother fled with him to San Felipe, and there they stayed while he grew up.

Then one day his mother said, "These San Felipe people are not your kin. Kupa is your home, but your kin were all killed."

Hoboyak fell to thinking about this.

"I want to go to my home at Kupa," he told his mother.

So one night they stole away. His mother did not want him to go to Kupa, for she was afraid that he would be killed. They stopped at Saboba, but Hoboyak was restless and was not content to remain there. So again they left. One day while his mother pounded seeds to take with them on the next stage of their journey, Hoboyak slipped away by himself.

After running far away he found a bear's tracks. He tracked the bear and found it. They fought, the bear jumping repeatedly at the boy. But Hoboyak always stepped aside. At last, as the bear went by him, he drove an arrow into its heart and killed it. Then Hoboyak skinned the bear and took home its hide. When his mother saw it she was glad. Then Hoboyak told his mother to sit on the bear hide. As she did, it became a bear, and carried her for a way. Then Hoboyak stopped it and it became a hide again.

"We shall now go straight to Kupa," he told his mother. "With you and my bear we can kill many people. I am not afraid to attack anyone."

Two miles away from Kupa they camped. Each day Hoboyak went to a place near Warner's ranch, where women were gathering seeds, and each day that he went Hoboyak changed himself to appear differently. This made the women think that there were many men, instead of one. The news soon spread that Kupa was inhabited by the Cupeño again.

The surrounding tribes again planned to kill the Cupeño. They got together and went to Kupa, approaching a hut from which they had seen Hoboyak leave the day before. They crept along slowly and cautiously, since they knew not just how many were in this hut. Hoboyak saw them. He went to meet them, carrying his bear skin. When close enough he slung the bear skin at them. It became a real bear and attacked them. While they fought off the attacking bear, Hoboyak shot them all down.

Then Hoboyak and his mother moved to Kupa. Later he married two Luiseño sisters and from this marriage came the Cupeño of today.

THE ADVENTUROUS BROTHER
[As told by the western Mono indians of Madera county]

Once upon a time there lived in Owens valley, east of the Sierra Nevada mountains, two brothers, Haininu and Baumegesu. Haininu was always doing things just for the spirit of adventure.

One day while he and his brother sat beside a lake they saw a water baby, a sort of fairy. Haininu threw a stone at the water baby. Immediately the water from the lake rose up and sought to cover Haininu. But he jumped from one rock to the other, going higher each time. The water pursued him, and just as he reached the sky, it touched him. But Haininu made a hole in the sky and staggered in, half of his body wet. The water had failed and it went back. So Haininu came down to the lake and killed the water baby.

Then the two brothers set out for another village. While descending a hill they saw Bear swinging on a sapling at the bottom of the hill.

"That is our aunt having a good time on the tree," said Baumegesu.

"I think I'll go down and see her," said Haininu.

So he went down to Bear.

"Let me try," he said to her.

Bear replied, "All right."

Bear then got off the tree and Haininu sat down. Bear swung him up and down, a little higher each time. When she had him rising very high with each upward movement of the sapling, she suddenly let go the tree. Haininu flew up far into the sky. As he was falling down he said to himself, "Sandy place." So when he struck the earth he fell into soft sand and was not killed.

He arose from the sand and approached Bear again. "You get on," he said. "I'll swing you."

Bear got on the tree and Haininu swung her up and down. Suddenly he let go of the tree and Bear shot far up into the sky. As she was falling down, Haininu said to himself, "Hit the ground." She did and was killed by the fall. Haininu then returned to his brother and the two went on.

While crossing the Sierra Nevada mountains they stopped to rest. Baumegesu pointed down the mountains.

"There are the Winds. They are our aunts."

"I'll go down and see our aunts," Haininu said.

"All right," Baumegesu answered. "Get a lunch from them, but don't tease them."

"All right," replied Haininu.

When Haininu arrived at the home of the Winds he found them making baskets outside.

"Hello," called out Haininu.

"Hello," the Winds replied. "Whither are you going?"

"I am going down to the plains, whence I'll never return," Haininu answered. "I have come down to get a lunch from you."

One Wind laid down her basket and entered her house, where she got some seed meal. She put this in a bag and gave it to Haininu.

"Drink water with it. That's all," she said.

But while she had been in the house getting the seed meal Haininu had made holes in her basket. As soon as he had left with the bag of seeds the Wind picked up her basket and discovered it full of holes. She was furiously angry.

"We'll kill him!" she cried.

All the Winds started after Haininu. They roared as they chased him, and pulled up trees, and brushes, and rocks, which they threw at him. He escaped each time. Finally he hid in a cave among the rocks. The Winds hurled a great tree at him, but could not reach him. Then they gave up the chase and returned to their house. Haininu left the cave, then, and returned to his brother. He got his bow and some arrows and went

back to the Winds' house and killed all of them. The
Winds' children, however, went into holes and he could
not get at them to shoot them. Only Winds' children
blow in the world today, and the caves in the mountain
passes are their homes.

Then Haininu returned to his brother.

"I did not send you to kill our aunts," Baumegesu
scolded. "You are always getting into mischief. We
will travel now."

They had not gone far before Baumegesu stopped
and pointed to a house in the distance.

"My younger brother, you go to our aunts living
over there and try to get a basket from them," he said.

When Haininu came up to the house he discovered
that these aunts were Rattlesnakes.

To Haininu's request they responded, "Yes, nephew,
we have baskets for you here. Let us enter and seek a
good one."

They selected their best basket and gave it to
Haininu.

"This is the best we could do, nephew," they said.

So Haininu departed with the basket, and the aunts
sat down to resume work on the baskets they were making.

"What's the matter with this basket?" asked one of
them. "It is full of holes."

"Mine, too," said another.

Then they discovered that Haininu had been up to
mischief when their backs were turned.

"We will cut across here and get ahead of our
nephew before he gets far up the road," they said.
"We'll punish him for this."

They ran quickly and hid themselves at a fork of the

trail ahead of Haininu. Then they waited for him to come up. As he passed each one bit him on the leg. Haininu felt sick, and he sat down on a rock. Soon his legs swelled and then he fainted. Baumegesu came to see what the trouble was. When he found Haininu in a dead faint he whipped his legs and the swelling went down. Haininu awoke.

"I told you not to do this thing," Baumegesu said. "You are always bothering our poor aunts."

Haininu ignored this reproof, and said, "You go ahead, brother, and I will follow shortly."

Then he ran back to the Rattlesnakes' house and shot them. One of the Rattlesnakes' children managed to get away.

As Haininu saw the escaping child, he said, "Well, I do not believe that you amount to anything, so I will let you go."

But that is the reason we still have rattlesnakes in the world, today.

When Haininu caught up with his brother, Baumegesu asked, "What have you been doing, now?"

"I went back and killed those old women," said Haininu. "They cannot get the best of me."

As the two brothers proceeded Haininu espied two Bears swinging on a tree. He said to them: "Friends, you are doing something fine there. Let me swing."

The Bears replied: "Yes, it is nice. You may swing." So they allowed Haininu to get on the tree, but when they had bent the sapling far down to the ground they quickly let go of it. Haininu was projected up into the air. Coming down he managed to alight feet first, although buried up to his neck in sand, and so avoided being hurt.

The Bears laughed and went into their house, leaving their cubs outside. Haininu proceeded to kill and skin the cubs. Then he took their flesh into the Bears' house.

"My father's sisters," he said, "here is some deer meat. Eat it."

As the Bears ate the meat they remarked: "It smells like our children, and it tastes like them." Thereupon they vomited what they had eaten, and then set out in pursuit of Haininu, who was running away.

When Haininu saw the Bears in pursuit of him he called to his brother, across the creek, and told him to put his leg over the creek so that the Bears might cross on it. Baumegesu did so, but when one Bear was half way over he withdrew his leg and she fell into the water and was drowned. One Bear was left and that is why there are still bears in this country today.

Then Haininu and Baumegesu started to return home. They built a house at Yuninau, a high hill, but Haininu did not like it and he left Baumegesu in it, while he went down to the plains. There he met with many more adventures. From that time on the two brothers were separated.

THE WOMAN WHO WAS NOT SATISFIED
[As told by the Yaudanchi indians of Tulare county]

One time a man and his wife started traveling. They had gone quite a distance by night time, and then they decided to camp in a cave until morning. They started a fire. They were both hungry, but there was no food in the cave. As they sat before the fire they heard the hoot of Hutulu, the horned owl.

"Call in the same way," the woman said to her husband. "The owl will then come and you can shoot him. We will eat him for our supper."

So the man got his bow and arrows ready. Then he called in the same way as the owl. The owl answered his call. The man continued to call, and each time he called the owl answered, coming nearer. At last it came into view and sat on a tree near the fire. The man lifted his bow and shot and killed it.

Then his wife said, "Call again. Another one will come."

So the man called again, and another owl came into view. He shot it, also.

Then he said, "It is enough now."

But his wife said, "No. Call again. We have had no meat for a long time. We shall want something to eat tomorrow as well as now, and if you call in the morning they will not come."

So the man, persuaded by his wife's words, called again. More owls came, and they did not stop coming. He started to shoot them. Soon all his arrows were gone, and still the owls came. They came, a great mass of them, slowly closer and closer. Then they attacked the couple. The man covered his wife with a basket, and then took burning sticks from the fire with which to fight off the owls. But the owls were too many. They overpowered the man and his wife and killed them both. And thus the owls avenged themselves for the death of their relatives.

Stories about Yosemite

Stories about Yosemite

THE CREATION OF YOSEMITE VALLEY
[As told by the southern Miwok indians of Mariposa county]

Half Dome lived with her husband, Washington Tower, on the bank of the Merced river. One day, she quarreled with her husband, and taking with her a basket of seeds and her baby in its cradle, she ran away to the east. As she fled up through the mountains she formed the upper part of the Merced river and Yosemite valley. She also scattered about many of the seeds which she carried in her basket. From these grew the various kinds of plants to be seen in the valley.

When Washington Tower discovered that his wife had left him, he cut for himself a white oak club and started after her. He soon overtook her and proceeded to whip her severely.

Half Dome, weeping bitterly as she received her punishment, threw the basket, which had held the seeds sown along the journey, to the north side of the canyon. It landed bottom upward and became North Dome. The baby cradle she threw over against the north wall of the canyon, where its arched hood or sunshade now appears in the Royal Arches.

Then Half Dome turned into a great peak where she stood. The dark-colored streaks on the wall of Half Dome are the tear stains on her face.

Washington Tower, having spent his wrath, departed and went over on the north side of the valley, where he has since remained, a great shaft of granite.

THE ORIGIN OF EL CAPITAN

[As told by the southern Miwok indians of Mariposa county]

El Capitan was a very small rock, a long time ago. At that time, it chanced that Bear and her two cubs one night lay down on it and went to sleep. But lo! and behold! When they opened their eyes in the morning they found themselves in a strange place. They looked all around them, and soon realized that El Capitan, upon which they had lain down, had grown to be very tall – so tall that it now reached into heaven. In fact, it had scraped past Moon.

Meanwhile, down in the valley, everyone was crying because of the plight which Bear and her two children were in. Then they all decided that some one should climb the rock and bring down Bear and her two cubs.

First Mouse tried, but he only managed to climb a handbreadth and then fell down. Next Rat tried. He too failed, climbing very little farther than Mouse. Raccoon climbed a little further but soon fell down, too. Then Grizzly Bear made a mighty leap far up the wall, but all in vain, for, like the others, he fell back. And after Grizzly Bear, Mountain Lion tried, but failed also.

Then Measuring Worm came along. Insignificant and small as he was, he attempted to climb the rock. Step by step, a little at a time, he measured his way up. A whole snow [winter] passed and still he persevered. Soon he disappeared from sight, and at last reached the top, but only to find that Bear and her two children had starved to death.

He gathered their bones and brought them down and the people burned them in the usual way.

THE SPIRITS OF YOSEMITE FALLS

[As told by the southern Miwok indians of Mariposa county]

A long time ago there used to be a village near the foot of Yosemite Falls. One day, a maiden from this village went to the stream for a basket of water. When she dipped her basket into the stream she brought it up full of snakes, instead of water as usual. So she went a little bit farther upstream and dipped her basket again. Again she brought it up full of snakes. Each time she went a little higher upstream and each time her basket filled with snakes.

Soon she reached the fast-rushing waters at the foot of Yosemite Falls, and then suddenly a violent wind blew her into it. While being tossed around in the pool she gave birth to a child.

The wind subsided and she managed to reach shore. Covering the baby with a blanket she went home. She would allow no one to see the baby, for it was a super-natural baby. But her mother, who had become very curious, took the blanket off and looked at the baby. Immediately a violent gale arose and blew the entire village and people into the same pool the girl had been blown into. Nothing has ever been seen or heard of them since.

The Poloti, a group of dangerous spirit women, live in the Yosemite Falls. It is believed these spirits were the cause of the disappearance of the village.

Miscellaneous

Miscellaneous

HOW GROUND SQUIRREL STOLE OBSIDIAN
[As told by the Shasta indians of Siskiyou county]

In the days when the "first people" lived they used to go hunting with arrows that had pine bark points. They did not know where to get obsidian, or they would have used that for points; for the obsidian made a sharp, deadly point which always killed the animal shot with it. The bark point was not so sure a weapon. Ground Squirrel was the only one who knew where to obtain obsidian. He knew that Obsidian-Old-Man lived on Medicine Lake. So one day he set out to steal some obsidian. He took with him a basket filled with roots. Arrived at Obsidian-Old-Man's house he went in and offered the old man some of his roots to eat. Obsidian-Old-Man liked them so much that he sent Ground Squirrel out to get more. While Ground Squirrel was digging in the ground for roots, Grizzly Bear came along.

"Sit down," Grizzly Bear said. "Let me sit in your lap. Feed me those roots by the handful."

Ground Squirrel was very much afraid of huge Grizzly Bear, so he sat down as he was told, and fed Grizzly Bear. When he was through Grizzly Bear got up to leave.

"Obsidian-Old-Man's mother cleaned roots for some one," Grizzly Bear said, and went away.

Ground Squirrel returned to Obsidian-Old-Man.

But after Grizzly Bear had devoured so many roots, he had only a few for the old man.

These he gave to him, telling him how Grizzly Bear had robbed him of the roots, and also of what Grizzly Bear had called out when he departed. Obsidian-Old-Man was extremely angry because of the insult which Grizzly Bear had offered by mentioning his dead mother.

"Tomorrow, we will both go," he said.

So early next morning they set off. Obsidian-Old-Man hid near the place where Ground Squirrel started digging for roots, and watched. Soon Ground Squirrel's basket was filled, and then along came Grizzly Bear.

"You have dug all these for me," he said. "Sit down!"

Ground Squirrel sat down, as he had the day before, and fed Grizzly Bear roots by the handful. But just then Grizzly Bear saw Obsidian-Old-Man, who had drawn near. He got up to fight. But at each blow, a great slice of Grizzly Bear's flesh was cut off by the sharp obsidian on Obsidian-Old-Man. Grizzly Bear kept on fighting, till he was all cut to pieces, and then he fell dead. So Ground Squirrel and Obsidian-Old-Man went home and ate the roots and were happy.

Early next morning Obsidian-Old-Man was awakened by Ground Squirrel's groaning.

"I am sick. I am bruised because that great fellow sat upon me. Really, I am sick," he was groaning.

Obsidian-Old-Man was sorry for Ground Squirrel.

"I will go and get wood," he said to himself. "I'll watch him, for perhaps he is fooling me. These people are very clever."

So he went for wood.

On the way he thought, "I had better go back and look."

When he crept back softly and peeped in he saw Ground Squirrel lying there, groaning.

"He is really sick," Obsidian-Old-Man said to himself, and he went off in earnest this time for wood. But Ground Squirrel was very clever. He was fooling all the time. As soon as Obsidian-Old-Man had gotten far away, he got up and taking all the obsidian points, tied them up in a bundle, and ran off. As soon as Obsidian-Old-Man returned home he missed Ground Squirrel. He dropped the wood and ran after him. He had almost caught him, when Ground Squirrel ran into a hole in the ground. As he went he kicked the earth into the eyes of the old man, who was digging fast, trying to catch him. After awhile, Obsidian-Old-Man gave up, and went home. Ground Squirrel then came out at the other end of the hole, crossed the lake, and went home.

He emptied the bundle of points on the ground, and distributed them to everyone. All day long the people worked, tying them on to arrows. They threw away all the old bark points, and thenceforth when they went hunting they used the new arrowpoints, and so killed a great many deer.

LITTLE LIZARD KILLS GRIZZLY BEAR
[As told by the Shasta indians of Siskiyou county]

Grizzly Bear, one day, received a visit from Coyote. While the two sat talking, Little Lizard, a child whose father had died, came to the door of the house and looked in.

"Your father used to work and make all sorts of food," Grizzly Bear called to him.

Little Lizard ran back to his house, crying, for, among these people, to speak of a dead relative was a deadly insult. Arrived at his house he said to his mother, "Old woman, give me a knife." She sharpened a knife for him.

"Well, what are you going to do with a knife?" she asked.

"Give it to me!" he said. All evening he sat and sharpened it.

Then he set out for Grizzly Bear's house, arriving when all were asleep. He went in, and with his knife cut off Grizzly Bear's foot. Then he returned to his own house. For some time Grizzly Bear did not know that someone had cut off his foot. But soon it began to pain him.

He moaned, "A-a! Some one has cut off my foot."

Coyote, who was staying in Grizzly Bear's house overnight, awakened at this. He called out to the other people in the house.

"You people, there, did you hear? Some one is suffering."

All the Grizzly Bears then woke up. They knew that Little Lizard had done this.

"I am going over to see where that child is," said Coyote.

When he got to Little Lizard's house he found him cooking the foot.

"He suffers terribly," Coyote said to Little Lizard. "You are eating his foot, and he is talking about you, who cut off his foot. I am going back. I know that Grizzly Bear will come to you. He will ask you what he should do to you for having cut off his foot." Coyote then returned to Grizzly Bear.

"Oh, the poor child! I do not think that he did that. He lies warming his back at the fire." Grizzly Bear sent Coyote again. "Go after him and bring him here. I am going to ask him questions," he said.

So Coyote went and brought Little Lizard back to Grizzly Bear's house.

Grizzly Bear said to Little Lizard, "What shall I do to you? Shall I mash you with my foot?"

"No," Little Lizard said.

"Shall I swallow you?" Grizzly Bear then asked. And Little Lizard answered, "Yes."

So Grizzly Bear opened his mouth, and Little Lizard jumped in. Grizzly Bear shut his mouth quickly, intending to chew up Little Lizard, but Little Lizard had already slid down into Grizzly Bear's stomach. He had with him the sharp knife which he had taken so much time to sharpen. With this he began cutting Grizzly Bear's stomach, and Grizzly Bear soon died. Little Lizard carried the bear's skin home to show all what he had done to Grizzly Bear, who had insulted him.

SKUNK'S VICTORY

[As told by the Nisenan indians of Sacramento county]

There once lived two big Bear brothers, who were always killing people. One day Skunk decided to put an end to this wholesale murder, so he set out for the country where the two Bear brothers lived. He found the country full of bears, and the dance house, where the two Bear brothers lived, was guarded every night by a bird while the brothers slept.

Skunk then decided on his course of action. He hid himself under a log and began chirping and whistling to himself. The two Bear brothers, in their dance house, heard him and sent people out to catch him. But the people did not find him and returned. Skunk whistled and talked to himself again. The brothers sent people out once more, with orders to turn everything over. This time Skunk was discovered, and brought before the Bear brothers.

"Who are you?" they asked. "Why do you whisper and whistle?"

"I was whispering 'food' because I was hungry," Skunk answered. "I was whispering nothing bad."

They believed him and gave him food. Then the Bear brothers went to sleep. Overhead the bird sang while he guarded them. At last, however, the bird fell asleep. Skunk then took his spear and killed the two Bears. As he fled away the warning was given. All the bears gave chase, but Skunk shot them (with his scent) one after the other.

Thus did Skunk destroy the Bears who had done so much killing in the country.

THE ABDUCTION OF LADY PELICAN
[As told by the Lake Miwok indians of Lake county]

Lady Pelican was given a puberty dance on the occasion of her attaining womanhood, at which all the people at Middle Village [at the present site of Middletown] gathered. There was Coyote and his wife, Frog Woman; Hawk Chief, who was Lady Pelican's husband; Grapevine Hawk, Hawk Chief's brother; Bluejay; Robin; Crested Bird; Humming Bird; and the two Snipe girls. For four days the people danced and made merry. Then they took Lady Pelican and shut her up for a month. After the month of confinement they took her out and put beads around her neck, on her wrists, and on her ankles.

The two Snipe girls, on their way to pick clover, saw her and stopped to speak to her.

"Oh, girls, where are you going?" Lady Pelican asked them.

"Come on with us," they replied. "We are out to pick clover."

"Oh, I want to come," she said.

"All right. Just bring your pack-basket. We'll pick the clover for you. Come along," the two Snipe girls said.

Lady Pelican said to her mother: "I want to go. I am going with them."

"Why, no," her mother answered. "You can't go like that. It's too soon after your puberty dance. Women never go about so soon."

At this Lady Pelican commenced crying. "I am going to go," she said.

"Very well, then," her mother replied. "But you Snipe girls, be sure to pick the clover for her."

"We will," they said, and they started out.

They found a meadow with clover, and the two Snipe girls picked the clover and filled the three baskets. Toward the middle of the afternoon the three girls started home. The two Snipe girls were walking ahead. They came to a turn in the trail, and disappeared behind a little hill. Pelican, following a little way behind, stopped when she saw a dead goose lying on the trail.

"Oh, I must take that home for a present to my uncles," she exclaimed. "They can use the feathers."

So she picked it up and tied it together and threw it into her pack-basket. Continuing along the trail, she came to the turn, and as she passed around it she felt her pack getting heavy. At each step she took it grew heavier and heavier. Then she heard a voice from somewhere.

"Hosh, hosh, hosh, hosh."

It came from inside the pack-basket.

Pelican's knees gave way. She dropped down to the ground.

"Lulut," it said again. "Hosh, hosh, hosh."

She wanted to rise, but she could not. Before her a strange person stood.

"Grandchild," he said, "I want those beads around your neck."

It was the Shoko. He began to dance around her. Pelican took off her beads and threw them at him. The Shoko caught the beads and started off, but he came back.

"Grandchild, I want those beads on your wrists," he said. "That's why I came back."

Again he danced around her, and Pelican threw the beads from her wrists at him. The Shoko caught the beads and started off, but again he came back.

"Grandchild, I want those beads on your ankles," he said. "That's why I came back."

So Pelican took the beads off her ankles and threw them to the Shoko. And still again Shoko came back, and said: "Grandchild, that skirt that you have on, I want it. That's why I came back."

Pelican had to take off her skirt and give it to Shoko, and then he went away. But even then he did not stay away. He returned after a while. This time he caught

her and held her under his arm and dragged her off
with him. He went to the north world with her, and
hid her in a pit under the wooden drum in the dance
house.

Back at Middle Village, everyone was questioning
the Snipe girls. "Where is your friend?" they asked them. "Didn't
she come home with you?"
"We don't know," the Snipe girls answered. "We
only heard her say: 'I must take this home as a present
to my uncles. They will be able to use the feathers.'"
Coyote then cried: "Oh, Bluejay, you brave man.
Come look for the wife of my grandson."
They all went, led by Bluejay, to the place where it
had happened.
"She is not dead," said Coyote. "Someone has kidnapped her."
Then they all set out for the north world. But as they
neared the boundary of the north world they could see
a line of fighting men on the watch, all ready with their
bows and arrows. The people from the south could
see that they would not be able to get across, but they
sent Little Owl, a great doctor, ahead. He flew over
the line and warned the people of the north that Coyote was coming on the morrow. So all the fighting men,
who had stayed on watch since Shoko brought his captive to the north world, were taken off their guard by
this information and they went to sleep with their
bows in their hands.
As soon as Coyote saw what had happened he placed
all of his people in the little sack he carried hanging
from his neck and went across the line into the north
world.

They found the north people asleep in their dance house. Coyote then took all his people out of the buckskin sack and turned them loose. The mice went around chewing the sinew wrappings of the arrowheads, and chewing the bowstrings, also. Others of Coyote's people tied together the hair of the sleeping people. Then they looked for Lady Pelican. They soon found her and all started to leave the dance house, stepping very carefully over the sleeping forms of the north people lying on the floor of the dance house. But the last man stumbled over the legs of the Crane brothers, who were sleeping across the threshold with their long legs stretched out.

The alarm was given! Everything was confusion. People were all tangled up because their hair was tied together. The fighting men could not use their bows and arrows because of what the mice had done. So Coyote from the south, and his people, got safely away with Lady Pelican.

Lady Pelican was very sick. They found that Shoko had bewitched her. He had made her become a fire-eater. Owl doctored her and after a while she was cured.

Thus was Lady Pelican saved.

GREAT WIND'S DAUGHTERS
[As told by the Shasta indians of Siskiyou county]

There once lived, on the top of Mount Shasta, Great Wind and her two daughters. These two daughters were very beautiful girls and many men attempted to climb to the top of the mountain in the hope of winning them. They all offered much money for the two girls. But Great Wind did not want her daughters to marry, so when she saw the men climbing the mountainside she blew them back. All around the foot of the mountain men were lying who had been blown down. One day, Eagle said, "I must try. I wonder if I cannot get there." He set out, singing as he went along. Coyote, who was setting snares for gophers, heard the singing. "It sounds like a song," he said. "Where is it that some one is talking?" The sound of the singing came nearer. Coyote looked all about. He saw Eagle coming his way. "Eagle! Where are you going?" he called. But Eagle went on. "I want to go, too!" said Coyote. "Wait for me." "Well, you can come, too," said Eagle.

So he put Coyote inside his shirt and they went thus together to buy Great Wind's daughters. As they came to the foot of the mountain and started to climb, Great Wind roared and blew. She tore open Eagle's shirt and blew out Coyote. But Eagle kept on.

Great Wind woman wore a skirt of hail, which rattled as she turned round. She blew very hard, and, although Eagle was blown quite a way down the mountainside, he came on up again. Finally he got very close to Great Wind's house, and soon managed to get up to the smokehole. Great Wind blew harder than ever in her frenzy to keep Eagle from entering. She blew him back many times, but he always returned.

Finally there came a lull in the wind, for Great Wind had exhausted herself. Eagle darted in through the smokehole and sat down. Great Wind saw this and she started to blow again. She lifted him off the ground where he sat, but she could do nothing with him. Finally she gave up.

Eagle was the only one who ever succeeded in reaching Great Wind's house to buy her daughters for wives.

LIZARD OUTWITS GRIZZLY BEAR

[As told by the northeastern Maidu indians of Plumas county]

There lived in the south many bad Grizzly Bears. They used to travel toward the north, where all kinds of people lived, and kill as many of them as they could. They kept doing this until they had killed all the people but two. These two were Lizard and his grandmother.

Lizard's grandmother would not allow him to go out anywhere for fear that he, too, would be killed. But one day Lizard slipped away and went to the edge of the valley. He took with him a small flint, shaped like a knife, and very sharp. While looking around he saw Grizzly Bear walking along in the middle of the valley. As he watched, Grizzly Bear stopped and started to dance.

So Lizard hid behind a rock and called out, "You big-headed thing, why are you dancing there? That valley does not belong to you, you big-rumped thing!"

When Grizzly Bear heard this he sat down and said to himself, "I wonder what that was that called out, and where it is. I thought that I had killed all the people about here."

He began to dance again, to see if he could make the person talk once more, so that he would be able to locate the voice. When Lizard saw Grizzly Bear starting to dance again, he called out to him again, as before. Grizzly Bear went up on the bluff, and hunted a long time. Finally he saw Lizard in a crack between two stones. He approached.

"Was it you that was shouting and calling me names, you little thing?" he roared at Lizard.

Lizard replied, "Yes."

Then Grizzly Bear answered, "People such as you have no right to be here. You will have to die. I don't want people like you around here."

Lizard felt for his flint knife, which he was hiding underneath his body. It was there. Then he got up on his hands and feet, and replied, "Well, kill me, then, if you want to."

Grizzly Bear jumped at him with his mouth open to swallow Lizard, but Lizard, quick as a flash, jumped down his throat, giving Grizzly Bear no chance to bite him. Once inside Bear he took his flint knife between his hands and began to cut Bear's insides. By and by Bear died. Lizard cut his way out of Grizzly Bear, and then stood and gazed at Bear.

"People here will not talk about you and say that you were a great man. They will not say that you killed all the people in this country."

Then Lizard cut out Bear's heart and went home to his grandmother.

BUTTERFLY-MAN

[As told by the northwestern Maidu indians of Plumas county]

A long time ago there lived an indian woman, who had a tiny baby. She used to carry the baby, tied in a cradle-board, with her when she went to gather food. One day while thus gathering food, a large, handsome butterfly passed by.

"You stay here, while I go and catch the butterfly," she said to her baby.

So she stuck the point of the cradle-board in the ground, and left the child. She ran after the butterfly, and chased it for a long time. She would almost catch it, and then just miss it. She had forgotten all about her child, and kept on chasing the butterfly until night came. Then she lay down under a tree and went to sleep. When she awakened in the morning, she found a man beside her.

"I am your butterfly," he told her. "You have followed me thus far, perhaps you would like to follow me always. If you would you must pass through many of my people."

The woman got up and followed Butterfly man. By this action she became his wife. They traveled, the two of them, for a long time, finally coming to a valley.

"No person has ever traveled through this valley," the man told his wife. "People die before they get through."

As they started through the valley, Butterfly-man said, "Keep tight hold of me and don't let go. Follow me closely and don't lose sight of me."

But when halfway through the valley they found themselves surrounded by a horde of butterflies. They were all handsome, and all wanted to get the woman for themselves.

For a long time the woman hung on to her husband, watching the handsome butterflies. But finally she let go of her husband, and tried to seize one of the butterflies.

She missed him and began to run after him. Then it seemed like there were thousands of others floating about; and she tried to seize, now one, now the other, but always failed. She struggled on, lost in the valley, and finally died. Her Butterfly husband reached the end of the valley and came to his home.

Now they say of this woman, who was not satisfied with what she had, that she lost her husband, and tried to get others, but lost them, and went crazy and died.

WHY OWLS LIVE AWAY FROM HUMAN BEINGS
[As told by the Wiyot indians of Humboldt county]

It happened a long time ago that in the family of Owl there was trouble. Owl was not bringing home food, and so his wife and the children were starving. They got thinner and thinner all the time. Owl left every day to fish and hunt, but he returned always empty-handed. At this time also, his wife began to notice that when she got up in the morning there were sores, as though from burning, on her body.

"I wonder what happens to me," she said.

Then she decided that her husband would bear watching. It was strange that he was getting so fat, when there was no food in the house, while she and the children got thinner. So one night she went to bed early, but not to sleep. When Owl thought she was fast asleep he got up and went out. He gathered wood and returned and made a fire. His wife watched all this, pretending to be asleep.

Owl took a piece of wood from the fire and burned her with it. He wanted to make sure that she was sleeping soundly. She did not move. She knew now how the sores came upon her body.

Then Owl reached over to where the stone mortar slab used in pounding food lay, and drew from under it all kinds of food, especially dry and fresh meat. He cooked some over the fire, and ate all he wanted. The rest he put back again, and arranged the stone in place in the same way it had been before.

He got into bed and slept until daybreak. Then he arose and went hunting. Soon after Owl's departure his wife and children got up.

"Get up and go wash your faces," Owl's wife said to her children. "I saw where the food lies, and I am going to begin cooking it. We are going to feast."

She went and lifted up the mortar and found plenty of food – ever so much. They all feasted and had plenty, and after, the children went out to play.

At noon their mother called to them again to come and feast.

Late in the afternoon their father returned from the hunt with nothing. The children were outside playing, and when they saw him approach empty-handed, they talked very badly to him. They could not forget how he had hidden the food and starved them. Owl went inside.

"What is the matter with them?" he asked his wife.

She turned to him and said: "I have something to say to you. Why do you burn me? Why do you starve us? Are you not ashamed? For I know now why you have done this."

Owl made no answer.

His wife continued: "Because you have treated us so you must go away and stay in a dark cavern, where people do not go. There you may talk."

And so Owl was forced, because of his wickedness, to go into a dark cavern to live. And that is why owls now live away from everyone, by themselves, talking to themselves.

WHY THERE ARE STORMS IN WINTER
[As told by the Achomawi indians of Shasta county]

Coyote and Cloud were going to run a race. But first they bet on the race. If Coyote won there was to be clear weather all the time, but if Cloud won there would be storms in winter.

So they started. Far away in the south they set out. Coyote took the lead very soon, and Cloud could not seem to overtake him, try as he would. So Cloud decided to use other means to beat Coyote. He caused fruits of all kinds to grow up in front of Coyote.

When Coyote saw all this fruit in front of him he wanted to stop. But first he looked back, and seeing Cloud far behind in the race felt safe and stopped to eat the fruit. So busy was he, eating the fruit, that he did not see Cloud come up and pass him. So Cloud won the race and that is why there are storms in winter.

ROBIN'S HUSBAND
[As told by the western Mono indians of Madera county]

Bluebird had two children, Coyote, a son, and Robin, a daughter. One day there came as a suitor for Robin's hand, Salamander. Bluebird was much pleased at this, but Robin herself did not like Salamander and would not consent to marry him. Coyote, her brother, was very glad that Robin did not want to marry Salamander, for he wanted her to marry Swallow. But to this Bluebird objected. Finally Coyote suggested that they draw straws to determine who, Salamander or Swallow, should marry Robin. This resulted in Salamander's winning; and although Robin hated him she had to marry him. Finding his wishes set at naught Coyote fell to planning a means of killing Salamander. Finally he hit upon a plan.

He said to Robin: "Tell Salamander that we are going to have a swim in the pool, and ask him to join us."

Poor Salamander did not know that the pool they were asking him to go swimming in was a hot spring, and, when his wife invited him to swim with her, he acquiesced.

"You jump in first," she said to him, when they arrived at the pool. "I shall follow."

He promptly jumped into the boiling water and was scalded to death.

Then Coyote joined his sister and asked: "What shall we tell our mother when we return without Salamander?"

They thought for a while, and then Coyote said: "Let us tell her that he has gone deer hunting."

When Robin returned home her mother asked her where her husband was.

"He has gone deer hunting and will be gone several months," she answered.

Bluebird, however, suspected something was wrong, but said nothing for she wanted to discover what had happened to Salamander.

When Robin's husband did not come back, suitors again came for the hand of Robin. There were Prairie Falcon and Rattlesnake. Prairie Falcon was very jealous of Rattlesnake, and he suggested to Robin that she get rid of Rattlesnake. So Robin took Rattlesnake to the hot spring and by the same subterfuge induced him to plunge in. He too was scalded to death.

When Bluebird heard of this, she was incensed. Even though she did not wish Rattlesnake for a son-in-law she did not approve of her daughter's way of getting rid of husbands and suitors, for she now realized that Salamander had met with the same fate. When she had spent her wrath on Robin, her daughter retorted: "Mother, what do you want me to do? Do you want me to marry my own brother?" Coyote who wanted to marry her, jumped up at this, and declared that he would marry her. So they married. Bluebird was so wrought up over the affair that she committed suicide by leaping into the hot spring.

When Prairie Falcon heard of this marriage of brother and sister, and knew that he had lost Robin, he sought them out and killed them.

THE FIRST POMO BEAR DOCTORS
[As told by the eastern Pomo indians of Lake county]

In the days before indians were upon the earth, birds and mammals were the human beings. There was a large village called Danoha [near the town of Upper Lake], where all the people were great hunters, not only pursuing their game with bows, arrows and spears, but chiefly setting snares in every direction about the village.

One day the people of Danoha found a large grizzly bear in one of their snares. Never before had such a large animal been caught. A great problem confronted them as they looked upon this prize capture and thought of the great feast it would furnish to the villagers. The problem was to get it to the village, for this was a large, heavy animal which they had captured in their snare. Each villager tried unsuccessfully to carry the bear, first on his right shoulder and then on his left. Bluejay, Hawk, Woodpecker, Moun-

tain Robin, Robin, and Grassbird all tried, but in vain.
Finally, a very small bird succeeded in carrying the
bear. He first tied its front and hind feet with a heavy
milkweed-fiber rope in such a manner as to enable him
to sling the carcass over his shoulder with the body resting upon his hip. No one else had thought of such a
method. The ingenuity of this bird, the smallest of
them all, won success and enabled him to walk away
easily with the heavy load. The others laughed up-
roariously, and shouted their approval of the feat, immediately naming him Grizzly-bear-you-carrier. Thus
he carried the grizzly home to the village, and Chief
Bluejay cut it up and divided the meat among all the
people. As a reward for his service this very small bird
was given the bearskin, which was considered a very
valuable present and worth many thousands of beads.

With this skin in his possession, Grizzly-bear-you-
carrier thought a great deal about the grizzly bear and
became very envious of his powers of endurance, his
ferocity, and his cunning. He forthwith began to study
how he might make some use of the skin to acquire
these powers. He needed an assistant, and finally took
his brother into his confidence.

The two went to a high mountain east of the village.
They then went down a very rugged canyon on the
mountain-side and finally came to a precipice, the bottom of which was inaccessible except by way of a large
standing tree, the upper branches of which just touched
its brink.

In a most secluded and sheltered spot at the foot of
this precipice they dug a cavern, which they screened
with boughs, so that it would be invisible even if a
chance hunter came that way. They dug an entrance

about two feet in diameter into the side of the bank for a distance of about six feet. This led slightly upward and into a good-sized chamber. The mouth of this entrance was so arranged as to appear as natural as possible. Some rocks were left to project and twigs were arranged to obscure it. As a further precaution against detection the brothers always walked upon rocks in order never to leave a footprint, in case anyone became curious about their movements. They even went so far as to have the rocks at the foot of the precipice, where they stepped from the branches of the tree, covered with leaves, which they were careful to adjust so as to obliterate the slightest vestige of their trail should anyone succeed in tracking them to this point. In this cave they began the manufacture of an outfit which would make Grizzly-bear-you-carrier look like a real bear.

The two worked thus in the cavern four months. Then the outfit for Grizzly-bear-you-carrier was done. He donned the bear dress and proceeded to act like a bear. He rose on all fours and shook himself after the fashion of a bear. He jumped about and started off in each of the four cardinal directions, in this order: south, east, north, and west. Each time he ran only a short distance, returning to the practice area for a new start. Finally, after the fifth time, he found that he could travel with great speed and perfect ease through thick brush and up steep mountain sides. In fact, he could move anywhere with as much ease as though he were on a level, open valley.

He repeated this ceremonial dressing and racing into the mountains for four days, returning each evening to the village and bringing the game he had killed while in his bear-dress.

On the fifth day, he again put on his ceremonial dress and went over to a creek, a considerable distance from his hiding place. Here he found a bear standing erect and eating berries. The bear attempted to escape, but Grizzly-bear-you-carrier gave chase and, because of his supernatural power, was able to tire and outdistance the bear, overtaking him at length and killing him with an elk-horn dagger, which was part of his outfit.

He returned and brought his brother, who tied the bear's legs together, as had Grizzly-bear-you-carrier, and carried the carcass to the village.

The brother skinned the bear and told the chief to call all the people into the dance-house to receive their portions of the meat. On the following day a great feast was celebrated, every one joining and providing a share of acorn mush, pinole, bread, and other foods.

The two brothers then announced that they were again going out to hunt. Instead, they really went to this secluded spot and made a second bear doctor's suit. This one was for the brother, who underwent the same training as Grizzly-bear-you-carrier.

Finally the two brothers started out one day, going up a creek. They had not gone far when they came upon Wolf deer hunting. They hid until the hunter came within about fifteen paces of them, and then sprang out and attacked him, the elder of the two bear doctors taking the lead. This hunter was followed at a distance by four companion hunters, and when the hunter saw the bears he made a great outcry to his comrades. After a short chase the bear doctors caught and killed him. They tore his body to pieces, just as bears would do, took his bow and arrows, and started off.

Meantime the other hunters hid and escaped the fate of their companion. After the bear doctors had departed, these four Wolf hunters gathered up the bones and whatever else they could find of the remains of their comrade and took them back to the village. The usual cremation rites were held, and the whole village was in special mourning on account of the fact that the hunter had been killed by bears.

The bear doctors went back to their hiding place, disrobed, and returned to the village as quickly as possible, arriving shortly after the four Wolves had brought in the remains of their comrade. They ate their supper and retired almost immediately, though they heard the people wailing in another part of the village. Their own relatives, the Birds, were not wailing, for they were not directly concerned, since the different groups of people lived in different parts of the village and were quite distinct one from another.

During the evening Chief Bluejay came in and told the brothers the news of the hunter's death, asking if they had heard anything of the manner of it.

They replied: "No; we know nothing of it. We went hunting, but saw nothing at all today. We retired early and have heard nothing about it."

Bluejay then said: "We must make up a collection of beads and give it to the dead man's relatives, so that they will not consider us unmindful of their sorrow and perhaps kill some one among us."

The bear doctors agreed to this and commended the chief for his good counsel. Accordingly, the next morning Bluejay addressed his people, saying: "Make a fire in the dance-house. Do not feel badly. Wake up early. That is what we must expect. We must all die

like the deer. After the fire is made in the dance-house
I will tell you what next to do."

Everyone contributed beads to be given as a death
offering to the relatives of the deceased. Bluejay himself contributed about ten thousand beads, and others
contributed various amounts, but the two bear doctors
contributed forty thousand beads. This very act made
the other people somewhat suspicious that these two
were concerned in some way with the death.

As was usual, under such circumstances, word was
sent to the Wolf people that the Birds would come over
two days hence with their gift. The Wolf chief accordingly told his people to go out and hunt, and to prepare
a feast for the Bird people for the occasion. On the
appointed day the beads were brought by the Bird
people to the house in which the deceased hunter had
formerly lived, the usual ceremonial presentation of
them to the mourners was performed, and the return
feast by the Wolves was spread near-by.

The next morning the two brothers again left the
village, saying that they were going hunting. They
went to their place of seclusion, donned their bear suits,
and again started out as bears. By this time they had
established regular secret trails leading to their hiding
place, and regular places on these trails where they
rested and ate. These trails led off in the four cardinal
directions, and when they put on their suits it was only
necessary to say in what direction they wished to go
and what they wished to do, and the suits would bear
them thither by magic.

Upon this occasion they went eastward, and finally,
in the late afternoon, met Wildcat carrying upon his
back a very heavy load. They immediately attacked

and killed him, but did not cut him to pieces as they had Wolf. It is a custom, even now, among bear doctors, never to tear to pieces or cut up the body of a victim who is known to have in his possession valuable property. Hence they stabbed Wildcat only twice. When they looked into the burden basket which he had been carrying they found a good supply of food and a large number of beads of various kinds. They took only the bag of beads, which one of them secreted inside his suit. Upon reaching their place of seclusion they removed their suits and were soon back in the village. After supper they again retired early.

Wildcat had been returning from a visit with friends in another village when the attack by the two "bears" took place. He had said that he would be absent only two nights. When at the end of four days he had not returned his relatives became anxious about him, and his brother and another man set out for the other village to ascertain whether he had been there or if something had befallen him on the way. They found that he had set out from the other village to return home on the day he had promised. Then they tracked him and found his dead body. They made a stretcher and carried the body home.

They arrived at the village about mid-afternoon, and when about a half mile off they commenced the death wail, thus notifying the village of their coming. The people came running out to meet them, and the first to arrive were the bear doctors, who immediately assisted in carrying the stretcher into the village. Every one wailed for the departed, but the two bear doctors were loudest in their lamentations. Also they contributed liberally, in fact, more than all the other people together, when the death offering was made up.

One day the two brothers left the village before daybreak, donned their bear suits and journeyed southward
to the Mount Kanaktai region. They made the journey
by way of the east shore of Clear Lake, Lower Lake,
and on down to near the present site of Middletown.
Here they found a hunting party setting deer snares.
One of these men was driving the deer up out of the
canyon toward the place where the snares had been set.
He saw the bear doctors and called out to his comrades:
"Look out for yourselves; there are two bears coming."
The hunters were up on the open, brushy mountain-
side. Two of them ran down the hill to a tree, but the
bear doctors reached it as soon as they, and, as they
started to ascend, attacked and killed the two, taking
their bows and arrows.

When the people heard of the killing of two more
hunters by two bears, they suspected the brothers, and
formulated a plan to spy on them. All were to go hunting and certain ones were to keep a close watch on these
two, and see just where they went and what they did.
They also discovered that the skins of the two bears
killed by the brothers were nowhere to be found in the
village.

So the chief called all the men to go on a deer hunt,
and all set off westward about midday to build a deer
fence and set snares around Tule Lake, for they knew
that many deer were feeding in the tule marsh there.
Nothing unusual happened that day, but after all had
left the village early the next morning, some children
who were playing about the village saw the two brothers, who had remained away from the hunt, giving
illness as their excuse, start off toward the east. Some
of the children stealthily followed them, while two

others ran over to Tule Lake to warn the hunters. About midday the hunters saw two bears coming toward them. Several of the best hunters hid at an advantageous point in the very thick brush and tule, while the others continued their shouting and beating the bush to drive the deer into the snares in order that the bear doctors would not suspect the trap that had been set for them. The hunters had agreed to act as though they did not know that the bear doctors were near, but if they were seen, to shout, "Two brother deer are coming," thus giving the hidden hunters notice of the approach of the bears. If deer only were seen, they were to shout, "The deer are coming!"

Finally, one of the hunters on the east side of the lake saw the bears and shouted, "Look out there; two brother deer are coming down the hill!" There were two trees standing some distance apart with a thick, brushy place on each side. One hunter hid behind each tree. A third hunter stood very close to a near-by opening in the deer fence and in plain sight of the bear doctors, who immediately made after him. The hunter was but a few feet from these trees when the bears came close to him, so he dodged between the trees and the bears followed.

Immediately the two hunters behind the trees attacked the bears from the rear with their clubs and jerked the masks from their heads. The other hunters came up armed with clubs, bows and arrows, and stones, and found the bear doctors standing very shamefacedly before their captors.

Every one shouted: "These are the two we suspected; we have them now." Some wanted to kill them immediately with clubs, others wanted to burn them alive, but the chief restrained them and insisted upon first questioning the bear doctors. They finally confessed to the murders, and took the hunters to their hiding place. Here they exposed their entire secret and told all the details of their work: how they dug the cavern, how they made the ceremonial outfits, and how they killed people. The hunters then stripped the bear doctors and took them, together with all their paraphernalia, and the property they had stolen, back to the village, placed them in their own house, tied them securely, and set fire to the house. Thus ended the bear doctors.

That is how the knowledge of this magic was acquired. It has been handed down to us by the teaching of these secrets to novices by the older bear doctors ever since.

LOVE MEDICINE
[As told by the Wiyot indians of Humboldt county]

There lived an indian woman and her husband. For a long time they were happy. Then the man ceased to be good to his wife. One time he went away and left her, and then she knew that he loved someone else.

"What shall I do to get him back?" she cried.

She decided to make medicine. Down to the water she went, and picked a single stalk of a cottonwood, which she placed in the ground in an upright position. That was her medicine. She sat with her feet at the edge of the water, and began to sing, weaving baskets the while. She sang of her husband, and hoped that the medicine would make him come back to her.

Ten days passed in this way, and then her husband came. She did not glance up again after she knew who it was approaching. He came right up to her and put his arm around her neck. She said nothing, but took hold of the cottonwood and hit him with it.

His heart was weak, and at this blow from his wife, he fainted. When he came back to consciousness, she demanded: "What are you doing here? I do not want you any more. You must go."

He answered: "I want to come back and live with you again."

But she said: "You did not treat me well. You left me."

"I will not do that any more," he said. "I would like to live with you again. I will pay you for having treated you so badly."

He paid her, and so they lived happily ever after.

Stories with European Motives

Stories with European Motives

COYOTE MEETS PITCH
[As told by the Shasta indians of Siskiyou county]

Coyote came along the road, and he saw Pitch.

"Luni, luni, luni," said Pitch.

"Where are you going?" asked Coyote.

Pitch did not answer. Coyote walked up to him.

"What is the matter with you? Didn't you hear me?" Pitch still did not answer. Then Coyote seized him and Pitch held him. His hand stuck to Pitch.

"Let me go, or I'll kick you," Coyote said.

Pitch did not answer and Coyote kicked him. The foot stuck to Pitch.

"Let me go, or I'll hit you with my hand, evil being," said he.

So he hit him, and was stuck for the third time.

"I'll kick you with my other foot," said Coyote.

He kicked him and this also stuck.

"I can kill anything, you evil being, with my tail."

So he struck him and his tail was caught.

"I can eat anything with my mouth. I will eat you."

Still Pitch did not answer to this.

So Coyote bit him, and his mouth was stuck and he could not breathe.

He called out, "Oh, my aunt, set fire to him. You are the only one who knows everything."

So the fire came and melted the pitch, and thus was Coyote set free.

FRUITO, THE GAMBLER

[As told by the Costanoan indians of Monterey county]

Fruito was an inveterate gambler. Sometimes he won and sometimes he lost. One night, after he had lost everything but his breech-cloth, he felt so angry that he went to the graveyard to see the capitan. While kneeling at the foot of a cross he heard a noise like a great number of rats, and then there came a great light and the capitan of the graveyard appeared. The capitan turned his back on Fruito, kneeling at the cross, and soon the light disappeared and with it the capitan.

"I wonder why he did not speak to me?" remarked Fruito.

The next night Fruito again went to the graveyard. He had gambled and lost again to the same man. When the capitan appeared Fruito said to him, "I came to speak to you. I want to get instructions from you how to beat this other man at gambling."

"Come tomorrow night," said the capitan, "and beside the gate you will find a little bone. If you have that you will always win. But now how are you going to pay me?"

"I will pay you with myself," said Fruito.

"Very well," replied the capitan. "When you are through, leave the bone where you found it."

So the next night Fruito came again to the graveyard and got the bone. Then he hunted up the other man, with whom he had gambled and lost everything. They spread out a blanket and started playing, and soon Fruito had all his opponent's goods – his clothes and his house.

A month passed, and Fruito made no attempt to pay the capitan for having brought him luck. One night, while he was sleeping, the capitan of the graveyard appeared to him.

"Let us go," he said.

"All right," said Fruito, "I'm ready to fulfill my agreement."

But first he went to see the padre.

"It's too late," said the padre. "You must do what you agreed."

And Fruito immediately died.

Index

Index